THOUGHTS OF LEAVING

THOUGHTS
of LEAVING

TESS HAMILTON

PERFECT
BALANCE
PUBLISHING

To my two daughters, who are my inspiration, my life, and forever will remain my reason for living.
To Lexie, my best friend, who believed in me, even when I did not.
To my one true love, who held my heart, who took my breath away, and gave me a reason to write this book.
Thank you

"Lift yourself high enough to see beyond horizons"

— RICHARD BACH

CHAPTER 1

*T*oday has brought new meaning into my life. It is my 60th birthday, and it seems at this age I should be at the end of my journey. However, a dashing cowboy has made me feel otherwise.

"Dine with me, Tess. I will buy you anything," he said. "I will buy you steak. I will buy you steak *and* lobster, I will buy you anything you want... just don't leave me!"

I reflect to a time when I was much younger, and no one ever wants to leave.

I RAN DOWN THE SANDY PATH LEADING TO THE BAY. THE ALAMEDA County Courthouse shimmered in the distance, along with the familiar echo of the seagulls above.

I ran to let go of all my frustrations. The home I grew up in was full of chaos and noise, and at sixteen and the sixth child in a family of nine, I longed for solitude.

As I ran, my mind was flooded with memories of my past. There seemed to be one in particular that weighed heavily on me. My youngest brother, Donald Earl, held that weight between his tiny little fingers. He was so small, and his image so large. I could almost hear his whisper in the air, as it danced by my ears. He passed away when he was two years old. I was a toddler of three, yet I clearly remembered the day he left us.

I was outside, playing jump rope in the driveway with neighborhood friends. My parent's station wagon approached our house.

It was a ticky-tacky neighborhood in the East Bay. We were divided by streets, that seemed more like boarders. Our small community was nestled right between Oakland and Hayward, California.

I watched the vehicle slow to a stop, and the tires rested upon the cement curb. Exhaust from the tail pipe coughed out black smoke, as the engine noise faded to silence. My father slowly walked around the family station wagon and gently opened the car door for Mother. She exited, and I noticed her hand, as it reached out and rested upon Father's palm. She was crying uncontrollably, while he comforted her. He pulled out a white handkerchief from his pocket, and ever so sweetly, wiped the tears from her eyes. They made their way up the concrete steps and opened our front door.

It all seemed unimportant, from my three-year-old eyes. I heard my sister calling me into the house, announcing to my **whole** world, my brother had died. I shrugged my shoulders and continued playing with my friends. My eyes repeated quick glances at the front porch, and somewhere deep in my cerebral mass, I had felt something was deeply wrong.

As I continued to run down the sandy path, I was riddled with pleasant and unpleasant thoughts from childhood. I was eager to move out. I wanted to be on my own. Clouds moved across the blue sky, and darkness settled against the cool sand beneath my feet. The bay area dampness had its way.

The night before Donald was buried, my father took me to the mortuary for a viewing of my brother. As I entered the room where

Donald was resting, I walked the long aisle before me. People were seated to the left of me, and people were seated to the right. Ahead lay my brother, in what appeared to be a white bassinet, covered with a sheer veil. I tightly held my father's hand. Father picked me up, drew back the veil to reveal Donald in a crisp white shirt, tie, and black suit. "This is not my brother," I declared. His cheeks were painted a rose color, his lips as red as blood. My eyes examined his hand, noticing the scar.

I recalled that it happened during our life in Lockwood Gardens. I was playing outside, and I remember my feet were bare. I was squatting, dirt beneath me, and wondered how it might taste. My little hand had scooped up a handful. I drew in the smell, my nostrils flaring, and I examined it with my tongue. I remember the gritty texture and the foul taste. I heard my mother calling out my name, requesting that I come into the house. As I stood, I felt my wet diaper hang down between my legs. The feeling of heavy feces lingered. I waddle up to the brick steps, and I made my way into the house.

Donald was playing with a toy truck. I towered before him; my eyes examining his toy, and that's when I made my move. I leaned forward and grabbed it from his hand. Donald did not waver. He immediately tightened up his little fist, and smacked me on the back, right between my shoulder blades. He had jammed his tiny finger in the truck hinge, and it bled. Donald never cried; however, I did. I cried over not getting my way and getting hit on the back.

"Yes," I said to myself, focusing on his finger. I looked up at my Father, with confirmation in my eyes and asked, "Why is he so still?"

"He is sleeping," Father said. "Donald will be sleeping a very long time."

So, it was then, as my father held me in his arms, I gazed upon my brother, without emotion, without tears, and I agreed, this indeed was my brother. I buried my face into my father's shoulder. My father's chest rose and fell while each breath increased in tempo, and then... he sobbed. He held me tight until it became difficult to breathe. The sound of my mother crying hovered in the background.

CHAPTER 2

*B*efore I was born, my father and mother were Salvation Army officers. They moved from state to state, until settling in California. I was born on February 12, 1956 in Alameda, California. We lived in the projects named Lockwood Gardens on 65th Avenue, in Oakland.

There was a clear division between colors of people back then. We were a white family, and Oakland was predominately black. We did not notice; kids never do. One day, my brothers and sisters brought home their classroom school pictures. I remember they each had a photo that portrayed the principal, teacher, and students, with a heading "First Grade, Second Grade," etc.

I remember the way my father reacted to each photo… there were his children, alongside all the other students. Our family, white, and all the other students, black. He was surprised.

It was not long afterwards that he and Mother purchased a home in San Leandro.

My father would share his dreams with me. He talked about owning an airplane, or owning a large sailboat. He would spend hours in our garage, making model airplanes and boats out of balsa wood. I imagined us flying high in the sky, or sailing far away at sea. He mesmerized me with his stories. He was so believable, so charming, and so imaginative.

I think my father wanted all of this so badly, that it drove him to a *very dark place*.

He was an accountant for a lumber company, and the sole supporter of our household. It must have weighed heavily on him.

Somehow, Father managed to purchase a light blue Stinson Voyager, with a beautiful wood propeller. It had a tiny little wheel, just below the tail, and two large wheels beneath the cockpit.

Shortly afterwards, Father announced that he was going to take us for a short scenic flight. He gathered up my brothers and sisters and piled them into our station wagon.

I ran around the house looking for my one and only pair of shoes, while Father sat in the car outside, with the engine running. Mother and I could not find them, and so I sat in the car barefoot.

Once we arrived at the airport, Father said that he wouldn't allow me to fly without shoes. I sat in the station wagon with my mother, watching my father taxi away with my brothers and sisters. My face pressed against the car window, crying hysterically I bawled, "Don't leave me Daddy!" My little hands pounded on the glass.

One evening, Father arrived home after a long day at work. He had a big wad of money in his hand. He hollered, "Come here everyone, I received my paycheck today, and I want to show you how much money I have!" He proceeded to display, the process of paying bills. I responded loudly, "We are rich, we are rich, look at all the money!"

My Father peeled off each bill into small piles. He explained, "This is for our mortgage payment, this is for the property taxes, property insurance, telephone, electricity, garbage service, water to drink and bathe, the newspaper boy, food so we may eat, automobile gasoline so we may drive, and this is what is left." As we all stood before our kitchen table, gazing at small individual stacks of money, I said, "We are poor again."

That was the moment I knew, if I really wanted something, I would need to work very hard, *nothing* would come easy.

The next morning, my father left for work, my brothers and sisters were shuffled off to school, and I remained home with Mother. The phone rang, and I remember the look on her face. She dropped the telephone receiver and cried uncontrollably. It was as though my brother had passed away again. She whispered the words, and I had no idea what their meaning was. Her voice cracked, "Father has been arrested, for *embezzlement.*"

Mother feverishly ran about, retrieving her car keys, and soon we were driving on the freeway. I sat in the back seat of our family station wagon, as my mother drove to downtown Oakland. He was being held in the big white Alameda County Courthouse. It had a large steeple, with a flag flowing on top. We entered the elevator and traveled all the way to the top floor.

I can still see my father, as he looked through a small window opening on the cell door. He looked down at me, and then over to my mother. He seemed ashamed. He spoke so sharply to her. His words continue to haunt me. "Why did you have to bring *her* here?" Then, so very slowly, he closed that tiny little door. The eerie creaking sound rang in my ears, and in a blink of an eye, I could hear him walk away, into his *darkness.*

CHAPTER 3

*M*y breath was heavy. I looked down at my feet, as I ran with one foot in front of the other. My pace slowed. I drew in the smell and tasted the salt from the San Francisco Bay. I inhaled the moist, oxygenated air. Run, I told myself, run until you reach the water. I glanced down at my sixteenth birthday, Adidas running shoes that Mother bought for me. I admired the three white stripes against the blue suede. "I love these," I whispered.

Then I sat. I sat for a very long time on the rocks that surround the cove. This was where I did my own dreaming. I dreamt about flying, as I wanted very much to fly far, far away. This place I jogged to was a bird sanctuary. Seagulls squawk all about, and I watched as they unfolded their wings; stretching, and reaching out as far as they could, all the while, moving their wing tips, as though they were gently playing a piano. The sounds of Leon Russell singing "A Song for You" came to mind. Someday, I told myself... someday I will fly.

I always loved the anticipation of taking off. While sitting on my sister's lap, in the back seat of father's airplane, we watched the San Francisco Bay swell, and the surrounding small towns that passed beneath us. With a solemn look on his face, and a tear running down his cheek, Father pointed at the clouds saying, "Look kids, Donald is up here, watching us."

~

FATHER WAS SENT TO SOLEDAD PRISON FOR A TERM OF TWO YEARS, AND my mother was beside herself. At my age of four, this seemed like an eternity. Mother elected to keep my two older brothers with her and send my three older sisters and me to Idaho. My oldest sister Katie was nine, Angelina was seven, and Jessica was six. Katie bared the responsibility for our safe journey, as we boarded a Greyhound bus from Oakland, California to Gooding, Idaho. We were about to begin a life with our grandparents; grandparents that I hardly knew and did not want to know. I only wanted my parents. I held on to my sister's dress tails as we made our journey to Idaho.

Idaho was covered in snow. Everything around us was white and cold. There was a biting chill in the air. I looked around at the acres of farmland that seem to go on for miles. No one had fences around their houses, and it seemed everyone had a basement. I recall stairs leading below the houses, with opened storm shutters. When closed, the shutters covered the entrances. There were a few scattered trees here and there, and if I closed my eyes and listened, the air held sounds of stillness. I wondered, "How is it that I ended up here?" My sisters seemed more at ease than I. We didn't talk much. I remained very quiet. I did not dare cry; it wouldn't bring back my parents.

They were gone, and it seemed as though, I was not wanted.

Living with my grandparents was different. My Grandfather, George, was my Father's Father. His wife was not my biological grandmother, but how was I to know? Lea was her name.

They were strange to me. Grandpa George hated cats. Grandma Lea was manly. They were country people. Grandpa wore jeans with suspenders, and Grandma wore jeans with suspenders. They both had plenty of flannel shirts, and they look just the same. Grandpa had eyeglasses, and Grandma did too. Sometimes it was hard to tell them apart, especially if I was looking at their backside.

They worked very hard around their farm. My sisters, and I, were put to work, and we were expected to carry our load. At bedtime, all four of us took a bath together. We were only allowed four inches of water, and when we finished, we weren't allowed to exit the bathtub, until we rinsed, and hung our wash cloths, neatly across the bathtub edge.

Mealtime was traumatic. We sat in the kitchen, around a wood table and chairs. There was a long kitchen counter, with a deep porcelain sink, and a window above it. The window looked out into the backyard. I wasn't tall enough to see out, but if I dared to stand on a chair, I could see all the way to California.

Opposite the sink was a wood-burning stove, with a chimney that ran up and through the ceiling. Grandpa would serve up our food from that stove. Piling food on our plates, he sat the plates in front of us, and said, "Eat up!" We were expected to eat everything, and it did not matter if we liked it or not. We had to eat it all. If we were seen putting our elbows on the table, grandfather would smack us across the arm with a butter knife. It would sting, and crying would make matters worse. My grandparents wanted to "Straighten us out." After all, we were *city kids,* and they felt we needed change. I was not sure what a city kid was, it just felt like I had entered a new world, with strange people.

Thinking back, and looking through the eyes of a four-year-old, what I needed most of all, was love. Oh, how I missed my father's smile, and the excitement of another story. I daydreamed about how he would hold me on his lap and sing; Little Boxes, little boxes. Pink boxes and blue boxes. Ticky-tacky boxes. I wondered; do we really all look the same?

Grandpa was nothing like that. Grandpa was stern, and Grandma was cold, just like the Idaho snow that chilled my toes.

Christmas morning came, and I felt emptiness. We had presents to open, presents that were sent from my Mother, not Santa Claus. He did not know where I was, I never told him. It was dark that Christmas morning. The sun had not risen, and I thought, "Why should I?" It felt like nighttime, not Christmas. I hoped I was dreaming, and when I had opened my sleepy eyes, I was told to get up and come to the living room.

The smell of pine wood burning in the fireplace, permeated the air, and the sound crackled and popped. The room was small. The large picture window overlooking the front yard looked like a gateway to *hopelessness.*

My sisters were seated on the couch, just below the window. They sat there in their pajamas, with sleepy looks on their faces, and their hands folded. Grandfather was seated in his easy chair.

Grandma urged me on, "Come on Tess, let's open gifts!"

Where are my Mother and brothers? How can we be separated, and enjoy this day? How can anyone be happy? My world was crushed, and I was the only one in the room that was mad, so I refused to speak. It was the only sense that I could control.

Cows surrounded me the day my grandmother took me to the dairy for milk. We made the trip; just the two of us. My sisters were enrolled in school, and I as usual, was too young.

Dairy cows fascinated me. My presence disrupted them. Grandma had two large stainless-steel containers filled with milk. As we left, the cows got overly excited, and made it difficult for the owners to milk them. Eventually, I wasn't allowed to enter the stable area. I was told to stay in the other room and wait while Grandma retrieved the milk. Once again, I felt shut out and alone.

Later that spring, I kneeled on the couch in the living room, gazing out the picture window at the flowers in bloom. As I stared out the window, I noticed a cat meandering through the yard. My grandfather was in his easy chair, reading. He did that a lot.

I made the mistake of saying, "Look at that pretty cat!"

My Grandfather bolted out of his chair and ran to the back porch where he kept his shotgun. In a blink of an eye, my grandfather shot that cat right before my eyes. He said, "Cat's kill birds."

And that was that, I never mentioned a cat sighting again. The event broke my heart.

One day, my sister, Katie, gathered my sisters and me together. We listened intently while she plotted our *escape*. She even drew out her route and plans on a piece of paper.

She said, "We can run."

We all wanted our mother again. There was a bit of hope until Grandma found the map. Katie was in big trouble and was instructed to sit in the corner. For—well, it seemed like an eternity to me.

That night at dinner, Grandfather prepared a meal for us, and once again it was food that I did not care for. I was defiant that evening, and I decided I was not going to eat the food on my plate. It was probably a steak, lined with gristle. I was always told to eat the fat. I would chew and chew, but found it so difficult to swallow. I was angry, and I felt trapped. All I wanted was to see, and feel my father's arms around me, to feel the touch of his hands, and see the warm smile between his dimples.

My Grandfather was frustrated with me. I was told I would sit at the table until I ate everything on my plate, even if it took all night.

After the family retired from the kitchen, there I sat. Dishes were washed, and I could hear the laughter of my sisters in the other room. The room slowly darkened, and soon I found myself sitting in darkness, staring at a cold plate of food. I was not going to eat, and nothing would make me consume the meal.

"Nothing," I told myself.

Where is my mother? I wanted her so badly, but I held back my tears. Shadowed in gloom, I inwardly seethed with hate.

There was no one to hold me, no one to love me, no one to comfort me.

Before long, I was told to go straight to bed without supper. I looked into my grandfather's eyes; the image of him, as he stared at me over the spectacles on the tip of his nose, charred my memory.

I was happy to go. I climbed into my bed and pulled the covers over my head. Shielded from those eyes, I finally released the tears, and cried myself to sleep.

❧

WE SPENT AN ENTIRE YEAR IN IDAHO, AND IT SEEMED LONGER THAN A lifetime.

My sisters and I hurried onto the Greyhound bus, bound for Oakland, California. Sounds from my grandparents' mouths seemed more like distant echo's. There was no love there. Love awaited me at home. The humming of our bus, along the interstate highway, lulled my sisters and I to sleep. A much-anticipated vision of our home danced in and out of my head.

We stood on the front porch, and pressed the door-bell above the mail slot, which read "mail." It was a metal door, just big enough for the mail-man to drop letters into.

I gazed at the yellow rose bush mother had planted, in honor of Donald. It rested to the right of the porch. It had grown, and I envied the flying bees buzzing about the bush. I peeked into the mail slot, when Martin opened the front door, and frowned. He was the oldest, and he appeared so grown up. He was ten years older than me, and that made him just about fifteen. Martin was always so serious, and he looked down at me, as though I did not fit into his world. My second oldest brother was Albert. Albert was a kind soul. I looked up at him and smiled. Albert smiled back at me, and I felt loved again.

Mother was disconnected. She always seemed quiet to me and refused to talk about my Father with us. In the evenings, I could hear her crying in her bedroom, with the door shut. She would lock it, so as not to be disturbed. My siblings and I would sit in front of the television, watching who knows what, and pretend we could not hear, but I always did. To this day, I have wondered about her mindset. My Mother was a proud woman, stubborn, yet gentle. I missed my Father, and I missed his energy. He was loud and boisterous.

Little boxes, little boxes, and we all lived in little boxes, little boxes made of ticky-tacky, and they all looked just the same; except ours was green.

I was home, and that was all that mattered to me. Idaho was behind me, and life had meaning again. I was about to start school. That was an exciting thought.

CHAPTER 4

ather moved to Oakland, California in 1943 from Blackfoot, Idaho. Mother also moved to Oakland in 1943, with her mother from Brookings, South Dakota. They were both enrolled at Fremont High School, to begin their senior year.

My father had the most beautiful blue eyes, and they complemented my mother's, a lovely hazel green. The moment Father saw my mother, he was smitten. It was love at first sight, or so they say. Father used to tell me how my mother was so cute. She was a small woman at only 4'10. She was bubbly with a great sense of humor, and had a smile that would shine, like my reflection in our toaster on the kitchen counter.

They began dating, and it wasn't long before they became man and wife.

Mother had wanted to become a schoolteacher. My Father told her, "Marry me and I will give you a whole classroom!" He kept his word, by fathering seven children. Although she always dreamed of becoming a teacher, she settled in as a mother and devoted wife. My father was everything to her; he was her world, her strength, and her salvation.

Father joined the Navy in 1944, and set sea on the SS John Dockweiler 2561, a Liberty Ship in the United States Navy. Father would deploy for three years, while Mother continued living with her mother, my grandma Flora, in Alameda, California. Father traveled across the world, enlisted as a Signalman First Class. It must have been a long three years for my mother, as she waited for his return. He was officially discharged on January 21, 1947.

After my father's return home, my parents relocated to Idaho. My Father enrolled in a private pilot training program in Twin Falls. He received his third-class pilot license, and began flying as a hobby, during the early years of my parents' marriage.

Years later, after my sister Jessica was born, my parents returned to California. My younger brother, Donald, and I were the only two children native to California.

I gazed at the San Francisco Bay and reminisced of my mother. She was so young when she married Father. He was eighteen, and she was a mere seventeen.

I examined her through a microscope. I analyzed her every motive. She was hesitant and could not make her own decisions. She depended on my father, in a way that I knew I could never be. Her struggle and sacrifice were too great. We came from two separate worlds.

I exhaled the cigarette smoke from my lungs, realizing the time. I had to get going; it was time to break from the memories and return home. Seagulls squawked, as did my heart. My feet moved gently into a slow pace. My mind stood still.

Father returned from Soledad State Prison just before I began my first grade at school. It was difficult for him though. He would hold my hand as we made our journey to Dayton Elementary School.

People would cross the street when they saw us approach them.

People reacted to my father; he was the *ex-convict*. I felt resentment towards those who reacted that way. They did not display happiness upon his return, nor did they know him, as I did.

Father helped me dress for school. We were poor, and clothes came into my world by way of *hand-me-downs*. Unfortunately, I was the smallest of the four girls. The clothes were usually too big.

My only dress to wear to school was a soft pink dress that mother purchased for my birthday. I washed my dress each day after school and then ironed it in the evening. I polished and taped the soles of my very worn, black patent-leather shoes with electrical tape. "No one will notice," I told myself. I came to accept this as part of my life in a big household. No one noticed, except my father. I did not complain to him, or anyone.

One morning, while Father was dressing me for school, he folded my socks over the toe of my foot, and pushed each foot into my shoes. It was uncomfortable while walking our usual route. I had a big lump under the ball of my feet.

When school was over, father stood waiting for me. I smiled at his arrival, and he held my hand for the short walk home. "Why are you taping the soles of your shoes?" he asked.

I just looked down, and did not answer, because I thought I was in trouble. As soon as we arrived at our home, father gathered me up, and away we went to our local Kinney's shoe store. He purchased a pair of Buster Brown saddle shoes. I thought the brown and beige were ugly.

"These will last forever," Father said with a gleam in his eye, and a smile upon his face. They would never match my soft pink dress, but I thanked Father. I sneered at my new shoes, while the shoe clerk disposed of my black, worn-out shoes; with electrical tape.

I attended school in a small community, referred as "The Washington Manor." It was a pleasant area to grow up in. I had many friends, and I enjoyed my studies and teachers.

My grammar school, junior high, and high school were within walking distance of my home. My community was nestled around all three schools. Everyone walked to school. Each morning, masses of kids walked down the street, alongside our house.

The grammar school had a foot bridge behind it that crossed over a creek. High school students would continue over the footbridge to their high school. I would admire the older kids. I wanted to be just like them someday.

My school had rows and rows of hallways leading to classrooms. I walked down each row, looking for my classroom number above the door. Each classroom had windows that ran down the length of the classroom, a big chalk board on another wall, and a sink to wash our hands in the back. Our teacher sat at a big desk in the front left corner. She gazed at us, as we each took our assigned seats, and scooted into a wooden desk with an attached chair.

I could see the playground outside the windows, and I would itch for the recess bell to ring, so I could run out and play tether ball. I was very short for my age, and I could smack that ball very high, making it impossible for my counterpart to win. It was usually some older boy showing off, and he would turn beat red, and storm away. I was generally, the only girl playing; I found it odd that the other girls preferred the swing set to tether ball.

I was a fast runner, and I passed the baton in relay races, as well as racing in the 50- and 100-yard dashes. It was not uncommon that I would *out run* other boys my age. I found myself competing after school, in many running and gymnastic events.

One day after school, our doorbell rang, and I ran to the door to see who was there. Expecting a human, I was surprised to find a bouquet, nicely placed in a blue Clorox bottle. An attached note had Tess printed neatly on it. I took the flowers into the house and slowly opened the note. It was written in many crayon colors, and said, "Roses are Red, Violets are Blue, your hair is like sunshine, and I Love You." It was signed by Bradley. I wrinkled my forehead and scratch my head. I could not understand why a boy would send this to me. I set the flowers in my room. My sisters teased me, and I was angry.

Not long after the flower delivery, I walked home on a sunny evening from my girlfriend's house. I would often play with her after school until dinnertime. I took my usual route, walking over the foot-bridge, just behind my school. School had been over for hours, but I came upon four older boys standing just beyond the bridge, smoking cigarettes. I recognized one boy; he was the older brother of my class-mate, Salena. The boys teased me about my soft pink dress, and my ugly saddle shoes. One boy grabbed me by the arm, while two others kicked my legs out from under me. I kicked and screamed while on the ground. Each boy had a hold of my ankles and arms. The boy, who I knew, told me to be quiet, and held his hand over my mouth, while he clenched my wrist.

I jerked about, and fought back with all my strength, and soon I kicked myself free. I must have looked like a mad hornet, or a crazy wild cat. I ran away. I ran as fast as I could to my home. Over my cries, I could hear the boys laughing behind me. My Buster Brown saddle shoes surely hurt those boys when I kicked them. I licked my lip and tasted the blood, and my knees were scrapped up pretty good.

I told my parents, when they arrived home from work, but for some reason my parents were reluctant to believe me. I felt they thought I provoked the boys, or I made up a story. The only counsel I was given was from Father, who told me to stay away from the bridge, and not to go there after school alone anymore. Nothing happened to the boys. I remembered my father's smile as he examined my new shoes; the shoes that saved me.

My junior high school years were the most difficult. I was becoming a young lady, and with that came those changes. There was this transition between one classroom to multiple rooms. We had lockers (something new), and we shuffled from teacher to teacher with each subject. I became combative and defiant, and I found myself being sent to the principal's office multiple times. I struggled with peer pressures and self-esteem. I wanted to be accepted by my Hispanic friends. I dyed my hair black, as though that would change my appearance. I smoked cigarettes and hung out at the local pizza parlor. A pool hall was nearby, and we hung out there as well. A white girl with blue eyes had a difficult time fitting in. I tried to look tough, and I managed to maneuver my way through this neighborhood of hoodlums, as my Father would call them.

It was during my freshman year in high school that I enrolled in sewing classes and quickly found that sewing came easy for me. One evening, while skimming through my *Seventeen Magazine*, I came across an advertisement. It announced the "Make it Yourself with Wool" design and fashion competition. The guidelines governed that 100% virgin wool was to be used in the creation. The garment was to be designed, sewn, and modeled by the contestant. The judged event would take place at the Fairmont Hotel. in San Francisco. I spoke with my sewing teacher, and she was thrilled to assist me in any way needed, allowing me to sew and design my dress in the classroom.

I selected dark blue virgin wool, with hot pink virgin wool contrast. My design would be sleeveless, with a high-neck, rolled collar, and fashionably short. I decided on an empire waistline, and an inseam belt that draped around my ribcage, fastening in the back. I chose an invisible zipper down the back. All buttons were instructed to be covered in wool, with bound buttonholes, and the garment required lining. I made the collar, the belt, and all buttons in the hot pink contrast.

When it came to accessorizing my creation, Mother and I purchased a navy blue 100% wool Fedora style hat from Macy's Department Store. It was perfect. I found a pair of navy-blue gloves, navy-blue platform shoes, and a pair of navy-blue opaque tights. I covered four small buttons with the pink fabric, and applied them along the wrist area, on each glove. I felt very chic.

Father, Mother and I drove to San Francisco for the event. The garment was delivered to the judges for examination and considera-tion of my entry. There was a nice restaurant in the Hotel, so we relaxed and enjoyed lunch before the fashion portion of the show.

Hours later, my garment was returned. I changed into my dress, hat, shoes and gloves, and my mother braided my hair in one long braid down my back. I entered the backstage, waiting for my turn to make the walk. The audience sat in folding chairs, facing the runway, as each contestant modeled their garment. I was nervous when my name was called, but I made the long walk down the runway. When I stopped to make my quarter turn, the loud cheers buoyed my confidence. Above all the noise, I heard my mother hollering my name and clapping. I was pretty sure she was the loudest of all.

I placed third, and received yards of fabric, sewing notions, and a one-year subscription to *Seventeen Magazine*. My parents were proud, and I was exhilarated.

We made our way back to the old familiar neighborhood. I sat in silence while looking out the back-seat window of Father's car, gazing down at the San Francisco Bay. As we drove across the Bay Bridge, I counted each undulation as we floated up and down, with the rhythm of the waves breaking beneath us. Beyond the rhythmic sounds, I heard my mother's voice quietly talking with Father.

We pulled up into our driveway of our ticky-tacky green house, I noticed our neighbor standing on his front lawn; his house was blue. He was a single father, with two small children. He stopped and watched me as I made my way into the house. His eyes locked onto mine.

CHAPTER 5

*J*anuary 1972, my family decided to host an exchange student from Brazil. Her name was Sofia Paulina Braga, and she was from Sao Paulo. I had no clue how to interact with a foreign exchange student, much less a person from another country. Our community, although in the Bay area, was still a small one. I was very sheltered from the world, and until that moment, I had no idea how big this world really was.

My sister, Jessica, and I were going to pick up Sofia upon her arrival. When our doorbell rang, I opened the door to a young man with captivating green eyes and a charming smile. His name was Andre Alioto. He was also Brazilian and had arrived a few weeks earlier. Both Father and Mother worked full time, so Andre, along with his American host parents, escorted us to San Francisco International Airport.

As we drove in their station wagon to the airport, I was fascinated with Andre. His accent, smile, charisma and sense of humor ensnared me. I found myself wanting to know more about this exotic person who sat in between Jessica and me. We arrived at the airport and waited in the terminal for my Brazilian sister's plane to land. Andre was comical, and he had us laughing and conversing comfortably. Time seem to stand still.

We were interrupted when Sofia's flight arrived, and a group of Brazilian students appeared, one by one, at the gate.

Finally, there she was; a small, shy Brazilian girl. She smiled easily, but she had some trouble conversing in English. It did not matter; Andre was there to help with translation. He really helped set her at ease. My eyes examined her, and I sensed she was afraid.

I took her hand and welcomed her to the United States. She seemed to relax at my coaxing. She was 15 years old, with long dark-brown hair, and appearing to have size five feet. I felt an immediate connection and thought, "This is going to be fun." I was always smaller than my older sisters, but I had a new sister just my size. She was my new, lifelong friend. At the time, I had no idea how important both she and Andre would become.

On the drive home with our new friends, the sky took on a grey color, softening with puffy clouds lingering about. Rain came down and rested on the agitated blue water beneath us. Sofia asked if the entire Bay Area was the city of San Francisco? As we made our way across the San Mateo Bridge, I surmised how she might have suspected that. The sound of thunder boomed in the far distance. The bay had captivated her, and Andre had captivated me.

We arrived at our ticky-tacky home, said goodbye to Andre and his host parents. I removed our dinner from the oven. Our trip to the airport was much longer than planned. The meat loaf and baked potatoes were overcooked and dry. Sofia must have thought this was the worst meal in the entire world, but she didn't complain.

I showed Sofia to her bedroom that she would share with Jessica. We retired early that night, and I heard the whimper of the scared young Brazilian student, as she cried herself to sleep. I somehow understood. It was most certainly difficult to be so far from your home.

Sofia was a wonderful addition. She settled in and became a unique part of our family; along with the help of her small green pocket dictionary. We used it constantly, looking up words in English and Portuguese. She attended our high school and made many friends with the other Brazilian exchange students. In turn, I made new friends as well.

Not long afterwards, Andre phoned to announce a Brazilian Carnival would be held in San Francisco. He insisted, "It will be on your birthday, Tess, and it is Carnival. You must go."

"Go for it," I told myself. *How can I not attend?* I decided to wear an extremely short black and grey empire dress, and my black platform shoes. I styled my hair, wearing it long with my bangs pulled back in a hair clip. My blonde hair complemented my inherited blue eyes. I was short, just like Sofia, and weighed all of 98 pounds. My small stature was accompanied by a huge amount of insecurity. I never considered myself beautiful. I was just me, a simple girl with lots of determination and imagination.

Andre, and his American host family, drove my sister Jessica, Sofia, and me to San Francisco. I was going into the unknown. I wondered, "What do they do at a Brazilian Carnival?"

We arrived at a large venue downtown. The night's atmosphere was illuminated with city lights and people. The temperature was cool, but nice for the month of February. My sister, Sofia, and I followed the crowds up the stairs and into the building. Andre's host family handed tickets to all of us. Upon entry, the Brazilian music echoed down the long hallway. I immediately fell in love with the rhythm of the Samba music. The drums, drums, and more drums pounded in my veins, and electrified my inner being. I could see the flashing of strobe lights in vibrant colors of orange, yellow, blue, and green.

Andre grabbed my hand and whisked me onto the dance floor. He twirled me around and around. We danced fast, and then we danced slow. Andre drew me in close to his body. He had a strong hold, and his strength far exceeded mine. His breath was heavy in my ear as he kissed my neck. He ran his hands through my long hair and explored me with his eyes. He kissed my lips softly at first, but his kisses grew more intense. I struggled to calm my Brazilian lover. Andre did not seem concerned with the audience that surrounded us. When my smile met his, I stopped resisting, and the room became still.

"I love you," Andre's mouth motioned. The music was so loud that I could only read his lips. No one had ever said this to me before, with such passion; It was February 12, 1972, and my 16th birthday. I was exhilarated, elevated, breathless and wanted so much to have this kind of affection.

Andre and I became close, very close. He called almost every evening, and we would converse on the phone for hours. He would arrange for rides to my home, or for me to his; that is until I received my drivers' license. We explored our local communities, and our eyes would explore our bodies.

We exchanged stories about our home life, and I was intrigued with our differences. Andre grew up in a wealthy lifestyle, the youngest of four boys. His father was from Italy, and his mother from France. He amazed me by fluently speaking four languages. His father spoke Italian, his mother French. They settled in Brazil and spoke Portuguese, and his English was perfect. What a captivating household that must have been. I deeply desired to experience the beautiful life he had. It was not a matter of if, but when; that, I was certain.

We would stretch out on a picnic blanket in a nearby park, and our youthful curiosity engaged us in a heated exchange of lust. I forgot about my family, my friends, and all that surrounded me. It was Andre, and nothing else existed.

"KEEP RUNNING," I WHISPERED. RUNNING HELPED WITH PROCESSING thoughts, feelings, and desires. The marina was a short distance from my home. It was the perfect place to run; it was lined with sailboats and yachts. It just happened to sit directly under the final flight path at Oakland International Airport. An inlet of salt water ran between us. There was a beautiful restaurant overlooking the bay called the Blue Dolphin. Alongside it, a pleasant sidewalk followed the edge of the Bay, intermittently lined with park benches.

~

I watched as he leaned next to my ear; his breath was heavy. "I want to marry you one day. I want you to be the mother of my children," Andre asserted. As we laid on the picnic blanket, our bodies exposed from the waist up, I looked in his eyes, and believed him. His mouth eased down my neck, slowly embracing my breasts, as sweat droplets circled my naval. My breath intensified, and I knew we must not go further. And then he stopped. He honored me too much to invade my youth. I was heated with desire, and I ached in places that were new to me. I searched his eyes. Were they green or were they brown? This thought intrigued me. We laid next to each other for quite some time and calmed ourselves down.

As we dressed and returned for home, Andre handed me his maroon sweater. "Keep it, Tess. When you hold it, you will think of me!" he said with a smile.

~

The Marina was calming as I watched the airplanes take off and land. I longed for freedom, and I longed for *him*.

CHAPTER 6

*A*s I sat on the bench gazing upward. The jet engines loudly hissed, announcing their final approach onto runway 30. I observed the flaps fully deployed. The belly of the aircraft dirty; landing gear down. I noticed the same configuration in a seagull just before landing; nose up, gear down and slow to rest just beyond the numbers. Flight is beauty in motion, containing a fine ingredient of exhilaration.

I pondered. Who was aboard the aircraft? Who were the passengers? Who sat in the cockpit? Were they aware I observed them?

I was so thirsty. I glanced over at the boats. The harbor housed beautiful boats of all varieties. The water slapped the pier, and the smell of the harbor was mesmerizing. When I closed my eyes, I could feel the moisture as it danced lightly onto the tips of my nostrils. I deeply breathed in, and I sensed a change in the weather.

ANDRE AND I SEEMED TO SPEND EVERY WAKING MOMENT TOGETHER. WE attended school festivities at his high school in Castro Valley and participated in functions at mine. We swam at the local swimming pool, playing endless water games while touching and kissing in the warm water that surrounded us.

We attended parties, went snow skiing in the Sierra Nevada Mountains, and walked hand in hand. We loved walking across the Golden Gate Bridge, ending with a walk down the "crookedest street" in the world, Lombard Street.

One day, while Andre was visiting in my home, he asked my mother if he could have my hand in marriage. My mother told him he must be crazy! She was probably correct. He must have been. After all, the insecurity I carried within me caused me to wonder who I would ever be good enough for?

Andre invited me to his Junior Prom. I was so happy! I said yes and planned the dress I would wear. I made most of my own clothes; I thought we all did? It was more affordable in the middle-class income community we lived in.

I selected a beautiful pattern for a straight blue satin lined gown with a green chiffon fabric over it. I made it sleeveless with a beaded V-Neck and empire waist line. I purchased white satin platform Mary Janes, and I had them dyed to match my dress. It was a lovely dress. I gazed at it in our full-length mirror; it would shimmer blue and green while I turned around.

I made an appointment with my sister, Angie, to style my hair at the salon she worked at. She cut my hair in a long shag hair style. It was a popular style that she called a "gypsy haircut." I was far from looking like a gypsy, but was pleased with her talents. Angie helped with my makeup as well.

I blushed when I noticed one of her coworkers watching us. His attention captivated my emotions. He was strikingly handsome, older, and a new measure of electricity sparked within me. I felt my fingertips tingle, along with a rise in my blood pressure. In some reserved way, I wanted him, and I did not understand why. I left the salon that day, feeling attractive and somewhat confused.

I shrugged my thoughts away. This was my first high school prom, and I was going with Andre! Little did I know, it not only was the first prom, but my last.

Andre arrived at my home, carrying a beautiful orchid corsage in his hand. We were to "double" with his classmate Dana, and his date; Dana drove his father's Cadillac and was waiting outside. Andre was so handsome in his black tuxedo. His sandy blonde hair looked great against his golden-brown skin. Andre was not a tall man, but he was tall enough for me.

We piled into the car and drove to the Claremont Hotel in Berkeley. The prom committee decorated the banquet room with bright-colored tablecloths, and vases of flowers placed perfectly centered on each table. A large dance floor featured a live band with big hair. It was electrifying.

Andre took my hand and escorted me into the beautiful place. His classmates checked me out. I noticed other girls whispering as we passed by. I imagined that they wondered who I was, and where I came from. I was a new face amongst students from another high school.

Dana and Andre found our assigned seats at a round table set with china, silverware, linen, and crystal glasses. We were seated for a "sit-down dinner" before the dancing began. Dana's date conversed with me, asking many questions. She was a nice girl, with short chestnut brown hair. She came from a wealthy family, just as Dana was. Dana's father was a well-known surgeon in the bay area.

I detected beautiful store-bought gowns and shoes much more expensive than mine. I sat quietly, my eyes scanning each table and each conversation. I marked the details of my counter parts; the expensive jewelry, the hairstyles, and the way they whispered to each other, while their eyes met mine in short glances. It didn't take long to realize; Andre's high school had a *higher standard* of students in attendance than mine. I felt awkward, and a bit out of place. However, Andre continued to treat me like a queen, as though he did not notice.

The pulsating groove of the 70s, the bold colors, and the innocence of my youth lured Andre and me onto the dance floor. We swayed back and forth with each beat, his body against mine, his grip strong, and his breath intense. Whenever the music broke, we kissed. Andre's Latin blood warmed his skin, and I almost felt the electric current between us. My connection with Brazil would be leaving soon when Andre and Sofia would depart for home. I could hardly believe that six months had passed.

My heart raced, my chest swelled, and my pulse seemed to flutter. I caught sight of shaggy brown hair with matching brown eyes. A desire from earlier events, from that day, stole a quick breath. I sensed that my heart had skipped a beat.

I LOOKED BACK ON A WARM TUESDAY EVENING. ANDRE AND I DROVE TO the local Drive-Inn theater in my father's Chevrolet Impala. We had pulled up to the car speakers and adjusted the box in the driver's window. We laughed at the "Redd's Tamale" commercial playing on the big screen.

I have no memory of the movie after that. We climbed into the back seat and began ripping our clothes off. We both carried on as though the outside world did not exist. We came so close that night. Andre had such a strength for resistance. Our undies remained on; however, hours had passed, and before we knew it; a knock on our car window startled us. We sat up and realized the entire inside windows of the car were fogged over. I rolled down the window, very slightly, and a man working there asked us to leave. The movie was over, all the other vehicles were gone, and we were the last patrons' there. I was so embarrassed and apologized. I felt ashamed. We quickly robed ourselves, and I started up the car; turning on my defrost fans and drove away.

I was glad we were interrupted. Andre treasured my virginity. There was a fear inside of me that would not allow him to feel otherwise. It became my secret and my virginity would not be revealed to Andre or anyone.

CHAPTER 7

My y exposure to Latin culture fed my appetite for adventure, but I was always hungry. I could not separate my very heart from them.

Andre and I lingered in the terminal gate at the San Francisco airport. I could not let go of him, and he held onto me. The gate attendant repeatedly asked Andre to board his flight. I wanted him to stay so badly, and I knew it would be years before we would meet again. I had to let him go. I watched as he disappeared down the corridor, and out of my world. I was unable to hold back my tears. I lost control and gasped for air. I turned to the nearest shoulder. Sofia did her best to comfort me.

I surfaced at my place in the marina. I drew in the oxygen, which allowed me to recover the wind that had left me.

The aircraft landed, and the loud sound of brakes hissing down the runway brought my attention back to life. I stared at the airplane making its way toward the gates. I imagined how slowly and accurately the pilot parked his ship; how it perfectly lined up with the gate entrance, and the ground crew, waving their bright orange batons, guided him in.

Reality set in, and I was alone. One by one, my Brazilian friends returned home. I looked down at my blue Adidas running shoes and pondered the unknown. What direction will I go? Maybe I should become a nurse? "Women do not fly airplanes," I told myself. I will become a nurse. That sounds good. I picked myself up off the bench, and I slid my hands down and over my hips. My feet moved to a faster tempo until I was running.

My older brothers and two oldest sisters left home, and one by one our family dwindled. Our time with Sofia passed much too quickly, and we yearned for another foreign exchange student.

My parents elected a South American again. This time she was from Bogota, Colombia. Her name was Luna Seguro. I looked forward to meeting another student from South America. I had a wonderful experience dabbling in Portuguese, and now I could look forward to a splash of Spanish. Luna was my age, and she was to live and attend school with us for one year.

I had enrolled myself in a vocational nursing assistant program. It was a "free" off-campus course held at another school, located in San Lorenzo. During my sophomore year, I attended class daily. I learned lifting techniques, bathing techniques, the correct way to make a hospital bed, charting patient data, and how to take vital signs. I learned medical shorthand, and medical terminology. I worked with patients in a local hospital, and I also had classroom time, learning vital functions of the human anatomy.

My classmates and I toured the nursing college in Oakland, near Lake Merritt. Presenting this to my parents, I shared my experience, accompanied with the tuition costs. It was not in their budget, and a nursing degree seemed further and further from my reach. However, while attending high school, I continued my education, and was awarded my NA certificate. Once acquired, the hospital I trained at hired me to work a PM shift.

My day began at 8:15 a.m. in high school, and then I would leave at 2:15 p.m. I had just enough time to go home, change into my uniform, and go to work. I worked full time from 3:00 p.m. to 11:30 p.m. I did my homework assignments during my thirty-minute dinner break. I continued this schedule for the next two years.

Thoughts of flying never escaped me. I discovered another "free" course offered at a nearby high school and enrolled myself in general aviation ground school. It was offered one night a week, and it would fit into my already crazy schedule. I lost myself in the principals of flight, navigation, weather, weight, and balance. When I looked around the classroom, I realized I was the only female student, not to mention the youngest. I often wondered why I chose the obvious difficult courses. I was, after all, a woman, and it was a man's world, wasn't it? It was awkward, and it wasn't long before I was completely lost. My high school schedule, along with a full-time job, made it nearly impossible for me to absorb the criteria. I discovered my weight and balance limit one evening and dropped the class. It was not yet my time to learn to fly.

Father was back to work, and had accepted an accounting position, with a CPA firm in Jack London Square. It was a quaint area of Oakland, surrounded by docks, and numerous ships of all sorts. Father would walk the square on his lunch hour, reminiscing about his flying days before his incarceration. However, somehow, he managed to purchase his second airplane. It was based in Hayward. I was delighted for him, and obviously for myself. Although, at times, I did wonder how that ferried over my getting a nursing degree?

Father fell in love with a Cessna-150 straight tail; it did not have a rear window, and only two seats. It was a high wing airplane, with tricycle landing gear. It was the perfect size, one seat for him, and one for me! I flew with him at every given opportunity. This seemed to satisfy my desire for flying, or maybe it fueled my desire? It was hard to know which.

I loved the exhilaration of rolling out on the runway before our takeoff. Sometimes, my father would let me take the control wheel, and I would gently rotate back as we ascended into the sky. Once airborne, and committed to our takeoff, I felt light as a bird; flying, climbing, and descending above the San Francisco Bay. We maneuvered over and around the horizon, pitching and banking through lazy eight turns. My imagination soared.

I timidly expressed my desire to become a pilot, someday? Father laughed, and said, "You are better off finding a good man to take care of you, Tess! Women don't fly," and then he winked.

I dismissed my thoughts and focused on his landing. I watched the wheels as my father made his final approach. The tires were so small. I peered out over my window's edge and surveyed as the wheel closed in on the runway. I said to my Father, "We are closer, closer, closer," and then... Bam. We touched down. I would blurt out, "Good landing, Dad!" We both smiled from ear to ear.

It was at those moments; our matching dimples were nearly impossible to hide.

CHAPTER 8

"*H*ello there," he said, as I sat down in the lunch cafeteria. Derk was a charming senior at my school. He was voted best looking of his class, and he was talking to me?

"Hello," I replied, as I looked around the table. Derk was striking and extremely shy. It must have taken so much inner strength to approach me! He was the popular football quarter back. I enjoyed meeting and getting to know him. We conversed throughout our lunch hour. He was aware of Andre, and the relationship we had.

It was to my surprise, as I later inquired around our school, my affair was common knowledge. The gossip chain had been in full force, and Andre's departure was not a secret. Derk was certainly not Andre, but I was lonely, and he was sweet. Timing is everything in life. It was time for me to move on, and start socializing with others in the community. Derk was a part of the community, my Brazilian lover was not.

Derk's Italian descent was hinted in his tall stature, broad shoulders, brown hair, and brown eyes. He had an older brother that was away in the Armed Services. Derk lived with his mother, who was divorced. He never spoke of his father, and I never asked. Derk lived in our ticky-tacky neighborhood, on the main boulevard.

He drove a red Volkswagen Beetle with ski racks mounted on the rear hood. He was an avid snow skier, and I got a kick out of him driving around town with his K-2 ski's, resting upon those racks. I think it was his way of being seen as a cool guy. He had a sparkle in his eyes, and when he smiled, he had one dimple in his chin.

Derk was very busy with school, work, and his social life. There were times when I did not hear from him. He seemed to disappear into the darkness and then reappear. I never asked him why I had not heard from him, because it did not matter. I was still lonely for the company of Andre, and no matter how delightful or handsome Derk seemed, he was not Andre.

When Derk was around, we hung out at the Foster Freeze, enjoying a burger and talking to our social groups. I was back on the scene with friends.

Luna, our exchange sister, was closer to my sister Jessica than me. I spent more and more time with Derk. He and Luna seemed to hit it off well, though. When Derk would visit my home, he would sit and talk with Luna. He loved her accent, and they would laugh and make jokes with each other. Images of Brazil, and my longing desire to be there muffled their laughter and conversations.

Once in a blue moon, Derk would borrow his mother's blue 1972 Pontiac Firebird, which fashioned a white leather top. It had white leather bucket seats and was fully automatic. He would pick me up for a date, and I momentarily felt special. I would wait for him to kiss me, hold my hand, or do something, but he would always hesitate. Our relationship seemed more like a friendship, and less like a romantic affair.

Until one-night, Derk came over to visit. He parked his VW alongside our house, just outside my bedroom window. It was late, and everyone had gone to bed, except me. I had already changed into my pajamas and robe. I recall the tapping on my window that caught my attention. I invited him in and his eyes scanned my attire. He seemed to see me as *his* innocent, naïve, fragile china doll. Derk wanted to tuck me into bed! That was strange, and with hesitation, I agreed. I took his hand and led him to my bedroom.

I snuggled into my bed as Derk pulled the covers up over my chest. I took his hands into mine and drew him in against me. I began undressing him by removing his shirt. He had the most magnificent body. The contour of his arms, the definition of his chest and abdomen, and the softness of his skin, motioned my senses to remove his blue jeans.

There he was, laying in just his whitey-tidies, when I heard my Mother's footsteps approaching my room. Derk grabbed his clothes and hid behind my bedroom door. My mother opened the door, and her eyes scanned my room. "Who are you talking to?" she asked. "Just reading out loud, Mother. I am having trouble falling asleep!" I responded.

There I was, staring at my mother, and there Derk was, standing in his skivvies, with his eyes wide open, staring at me! It was comical, and yet I had to remain still without emotion. With obvious resistance, my mother closed the door, and her footsteps faded into the silence. Derk remained frozen, and I began to giggle. He bolted from behind the door faster than a speeding bullet, trying to slip his jeans on; one leg at a time. He danced about the room, and I laid back and admired the view. Derk fled from my house, into the dark night. As I listened to his VW zoom down the boulevard, I pondered if I would ever see him again?

The community we lived in viewed us as the good-looking couple, and it wasn't long before Derk started showing up again. We fell back into our friendship-style dating. The downside to this seemed to discourage anyone else from asking me out. I had propositioned many guys at school, if they would escort me to our school prom, and they would decline. The common response was, "You are Derk's girlfriend, I can't go with you." My good-looking boyfriend was indeed popular, but definitely introverted.

That evening of the prom, I ended up hanging out with Derk in his VW, outside my house. We watched as couples drove by, heading to the prom. I recall passing a pipe over to Derk, while enjoying the calming effects of hashish. I sank back and thought of Andre. They were nothing alike.

Days passed, and it seemed everyone would call, except Derk. My parents would answer the phone, "Tess's house." Father and Mother used to get a big kick out of my social life.

It was a quiet evening and there I was, washing the supper dishes when the telephone rang. I sprang to answer it, and a woman asked for me. She introduced herself as the "Miss Washington Manor" beauty pageant planner, held annually at our community park. She asked if I would be interested in becoming a contestant. I was so surprised. I told her that I needed to ask my parents, and I would get back to her.

My mother was ecstatic! I think she lived out her fantasy life through me. She loved the idea of me being in a beauty pageant. I, on the other hand, was insecure and did not see myself as beautiful. I was the girl who loved working on cars, flying airplanes, and getting my hands dirty. The thought of walking down a runway, with just a swimsuit on, scared the you-know-what out of me. However, with much encouragement from my father and mother, I accepted the opportunity to participate.

I altered my sister Katie's pretty soft-pink prom dress to fit me. I produced a matching pink straw hat with a large brim and added a white pair of gloves. I borrowed a pair of hot-pink satin shoes from a high school classmate. I completed my look with a hand-held basket of white, pink, and hot-pink carnations.

The pageant took place on a beautiful summer day in 1972, at the Manor Park; referred to amongst the locals. Eleven contestants and I meandered about, talking with families and spectators. I passed out my flowers to those I conversed with, usually handing one to a small child who was curious enough to speak to me. The park was filled with booths, vendors, games, food, and picnic areas for families to congregate. The pageant attracted the biggest crowd for our small community.

Not long into the day, an announcement was made over the PA system, and all contestants were instructed to return to the outdoor stage, which was located in the center of the park. We entered the stage, and one by one we answered questions from a group of judges. We were then instructed to change for the swimsuit competition.

Oh, how awkward I felt. I chose a silver one-piece suit, even though most contestants had chosen a bikini. During my last-minute-shopping, I had found a faux-velvet suit on a bargain table. I casually slipped into my suit. The plunging neckline, with crisscross ties down the front, exposed my naval. My entire back was bare down to my buttock. The emphasis would be on my hips, bottom and legs, and not my chest.

As I scanned the dressing room, I noticed most contestants were much larger in the bust area than me. I was always too small, too young, too this, too that. I stepped into a borrowed pair of silver platform sandals and did one last check. It was the best that I could do, with the amount of time and money I could devote to my wardrobe.

The announcer called my name. I could hear the shouting and clapping for the prior contestant who had just returned from her swimsuit walk. She was beautiful, brunette, and very well endowed. I held up my chin, pulled back my shoulders, and then hesitated. I drew from deep within all the strength I had and walked out onto the stage in front of the crowd. I was terrified.

I recalled the fashion show in San Francisco and imagined myself wearing my wool dress. I forced a big smile and walked the walk, turning a quarter turn with each step. The crowd yelled, whistled, and clapped. Before I knew it, I was done. Once I was behind the stage, I let out a deep breath. "Ok," I told myself, "You did it."

One by one, each contestant made the walk. Each were greeted with cheering. It was a nice community. Everyone was kind and considerate. I think all of us felt accepted and appreciated, regardless of our beauty. In my mind, they were all beautiful. When I looked for Derk in the crowds, I did not see him. I wondered why he was not there? I thought he liked me. I thought he was my boyfriend? Then I chuckled; everyone else thought that.

My angst was interrupted, when there was an announcement requesting all contestants to return to the stage. It was time to announce the winner.

We had changed back into our gowns for the final portion of the pageant and gathered back on stage to hear who would be named the winner.

The announcer revealed the second runner-up was Susan Sanders. The crowd cheered. First runner-up was Lexie McLane. Again, the crowds cheered and stood. In my mind, I had chosen who I suspected would win, and I was hopeful. I was her biggest fan.

The winner was . . .

I thought I heard my name, but it only echoed in my mind. I repeated my name, "Tess?" over, and over. I stood motionless. The proclamation did not register. I was convinced it would not be me. The cheer from the audience failed to penetrate the thoughts in my head. The contestants gathered around me, hugging me; "Me" I said to myself. Susan, Lexie and I stood together as they crowned each of us one by one, while cameras flashed left and right.

It was like a dream. I was the winner, and now I had to make the walk.... the walk.... oh, the walk, with flowers in hand, a crown on my head, and a smile on my face. I surveyed the crowds, tears running down my cheeks. Father and Mother stood proudly cheering. Luna and Jessica standing and waving. Mother smiled from ear to ear. "That's my daughter!" she shouted. I was obviously living out my Mother's fantasies again. She was happy.

As the crowd dissipated, I continued my search for Derk. My eyes scanned the crowds of people. I noticed my ogling neighbor, with his two small children, holding up his 35 mm camera. I had smiled for the camera and then turned away. Some of our mutual friends said Derk, or Mr. Good-looking, was there for part of the event, but then he disappeared. I guess he did not want to hang around, just in case I lost.

My heart turned to Andre. He would have been there, I told myself. I looked up at the beautiful puffy clouds in the sky, squinted my eyes at the glow of the sun, and felt the slight ocean breeze brush my face. As I strolled out of the park area, Father honked the station wagon horn, and I smiled.

CHAPTER 9

"Sit up straight!" the words rang in my ears as I looked up at my stern typing teacher. He commanded that we sit upright, shoulders back, legs uncrossed, and our feet firmly planted on the floor. He paced up and down the rows of students as we pounded out typing lessons. Our classroom fashioned old manual typewriters with blank keys, and a return arm that protruded out from the left side. It was as though; we were typing in the blind. The sound of many keys clicking created a rhythmic cacophony.

He would stare and call out our names in an effort to embarrass us. Pausing alongside my typewriter, he looked me up and down, and said aloud, "Who do you think you are, Cleopatra?" Briefly, I glimpsed my grandfather looking from behind the eyes of my teacher. A butter knife smacked my arm, almost as hard as my teachers' words. I hated typing, and I hated him.

He failed to appreciate my chosen outfit that day. It was *hot pants* era, and I took full liberty of living on the edge. He sent me to the dean's office many times, complaining about my clothes, or lack thereof. Like my grandfather, I think my typing teacher did not care for me; it was that simple.

I struggled between work and classes, but I did manage to save my money. I decided to put all my earnings into a bank account, and when I graduated from high school, I planned to fly to Brazil. I put nursing aside and focused on Andre. I knew he would want me, and life would be perfect again.

Over the years, I had taken on so many classes that I had earned enough credits to graduate in early January 1974, rather than in June. I chose not to participate in the usual graduation events that occurred during the latter part of my senior year. I was in a hurry, and maybe later I would regret it. It had been two years since Andre left, and for me that seemed like an eternity. It was a reminder of years separated from my father. I missed Andre, so I focused on seeing him again.

THOUGHTS FLOODED MY MIND AS I POUNDED THE PATH TO THE BAY. I calculated costs and time of departure. I wanted nothing more. My brain continued to race between this and that. Thoughts of typing waned from my mind, and thoughts of my little brother Donald waxed in. He was so good. Father told me he was their angel.

I was their devil child. Donald didn't give them any trouble; he behaved well and was the apple of my father's eye. My mother loved her sons most. After Donald died, Albert became the favorite. She didn't hide it well. It was apparent in the way she spoke. My oldest brother Martin knew this, and it always troubled him.

Martin and Father were at constant opposing positions. There was one evening, in particular, that my brother had become very defiant. They were in the kitchen, and I heard my father shouting, "I will pack your bags, and set them on the porch, then I'll kick you in the ass on your way out!" Martin was riding motorcycles, sporting leather coats, and a waterfall hair style fashioned a bit like James Dean. Martin was tough, and Father was frustrated. I was eight at the time, and ran to my brother's rescue. I shouted at my father, "Leave my brother alone!" They both snapped their heads in my direction, and just growled at me.

Martin was handsome, and he seemed very tall in my mind. He

had light brown hair and blue eyes. He was cool, and he hung out with a wild bunch. I could hear him riding up the street, and into our driveway on his motorcycle, with "butter-fly" handle bars. He would wind up the engine before shutting down, and I would run outside and beg him for a ride. He would look down at me and shake his head no. I would stomp off upset until one day he nodded his head yes. Martin lifted me up onto the back of his bike, and away we went. It was a short ride, up and down the street, but I still smiled from ear to ear. He made my day.

Martin eventually packed his suitcase and enlisted in the US Navy. He was sent to Japan. It was good for Martin. He needed some structure. Being the oldest, he was subject to all the problems in our household. He remained with mother, when I was sent away. There will always be that dense black hole in time. It surely weighed heavily on Martin, as did me. I loved him, but never really knew him. He did not talk much to me. I was in the way most of the time.

THE MEMORIES OF BOTH BROTHERS FADED AS I SAT AND WATCHED THE seagulls. It was my birthday, and I finally reached 18. The soft music playing from a nearby boat sang out Joe Cocker's, "You are so Beautiful." I closed my eyes and took in the lyrics. My breathing slowed as I anticipated my evening. A birthday dinner was planned that night. I sat back, and slowly opened my eyes just in time to admire a seagull take flight, "I wondered. Should I reconsider going to Brazil?"

It was earlier that morning when I had entered the Pan American Airlines building in downtown Oakland; I was nervous. The large building in the heart of Oakland penetrated a beacon of salvation. It stood tall like the control tower at the north end of the runway. I had cash to purchase my very own round-trip ticket to South America. I anxiously clasped the required $937.00 that took years to save.

As I stood in line, waiting for a ticket agent to help me, I looked out the large picture windows. A perfect view of the Alameda County Courthouse came into focus. I saw the white steeple and the American flag mounted perfectly centered, right on top. The flag rippled in the wind, and I thought of my father.

The memory of his eyes, his sadness, his rejection brought anguish, and I tried to dismiss them but could not. I scanned the lawn outside the building, and I recalled my mother and all of us, sitting on a blanket enjoying a picnic lunch. We sat there so father could watch us from his cell. It must have crushed him to see us laughing, eating, and relaxing on that green lawn.

Father was always the imaginary and inventor in our household. His writings, his tinkering, his ability to see beyond the end of our horizons, gave me hope. I refused to let go of that. I would watch as he repaired and made new of old things.

I remember when a timer came into our life. Father was fascinated with this device. He would plug the timer into an electrical outlet, and experiment. "Hum... let's see what we can do with this?" he would say. It was not long before Father decided he could plug the coffee pot into a timer, and coffee would begin to perk just before his awakening. I thought it was remarkable! We began having timers popping up all over our home. I would walk into the bathroom first thing in the morning, and a timer would have music playing for our comfort. Our lamps in the family room would go on just around dusk. Our Christmas tree would light at dark, and I would marvel. "He was a genius," I would tell myself.

"Can I help you?" the ticket agent asked. I looked up at his smiling face and shook the memories. I approached the counter, eager to purchase my freedom. The agent handed me the tickets and smiled, "Have a great trip Tess! How exciting!" I thanked him and as I left the building, I took one more glance at that American flag.

I HAD ACQUIRED MY PASSPORT, RECEIVED ALL IMMUNIZATIONS (PER federal regulation), and was ready to go. Or was I?

I was going to live with Sofia and her family for six months, and

Luna for one. Andre had no idea I was coming. It would either be a good surprise, or the biggest mistake of my life.

I took in a deep breath of the salty air and brushed a stray hair from my face. I smiled, and I thought, "I wonder if I will ever run this path again?"

I glanced up at the cloudy day, and at the Bay Bridge in the distance. The skyline of Oakland had its beauty. Despite all the separation of color, there was only one color that day; the sky... and it was blue.

CHAPTER 10

"*H*ey, Hamilton. I need your help!" He called to me from inside his hospital room. It was during my senior year in high school that I was assigned the west wing. I had 30 patients to care for, including the pleasant Mr. Shell. The nice old man needed my assistance getting into bed.

My patients addressed me by my last name except for one woman. Her name was Gretchen. Gretchen sang each time I entered her room. She sang the same song that my father sang to me when I was a child. "Little Boxes, Little Boxes." I laughed and sang along with her. She was charming, but she, along with all my other patients, was lonely. They seldom had visitors. The loneliness was palpable, weighing on them from within their soul. I wanted to bring a bit of sunlight into their lives.

"Let's get you into bed, Mr. Shell," I said. Mr. Shell expressed his concern about his roommate, Ben Walters. "He's been in the restroom a very long time," he squeaked.

Ben was a very self-sufficient tall and large black man. He was quiet and kept to himself most of the time. "Let's give him his privacy," I said to Mr. Shell. "I will check on him in a few more minutes."

However, Mr. Shell persisted, and I decided to enter the restroom to check on Ben.

I spied Ben's legs and could see that he sat on the commode. I kept the door partly closed, and I called out his name. Ben did not answer, so I decided to enter the restroom and help him.

It was too late. Ben had expired. I called out to the nursing staff, "Code blue in room 226." My immediate supervisor, the RN on duty, came running into the room. Together we managed to lay Ben down on to the floor and began CPR.

Poor Mr. Shell laid in bed watching as we both worked on Ben for what seemed like hours. It was no use; we could not revive him. Ben was pronounced dead.

It was my first experience having a patient expire on my shift. I wished I could say it was the last. Many would follow over my two years working there. It became part of nursing, but some patients never leave.

There was Mr. Roach. He looked like he smoked a few in his day. The brown nicotine stains between his first two fingers was a dead giveaway. He sat in his wheelchair at the nursing station from sun up to sun down, calling out for a cigarette. He was allowed one cigarette each hour. He sucked down his allowance, inhaling as if he was smoking a joint. The cigarette burned fast and hot. In less than two minutes, he finished the smoke and he would start in again, "Nurse, can I have a cigarette?"

I loved the speedy Mr. Collins. After the dinner hour, he would advance into his wheelchair, and away he went. He flew down the hallways with the Steve McQueen like speed. If I spied him approaching, I moved out of his way. As he soared by, he had the biggest grin on his face. I often wondered why he didn't walk, because his legs moved faster than mine.

The hospital was a waiting place. It was a place between our past and our future. People waiting to pass on and making the best of being forgotten. Before Ben died, he told me, "Find someone to love and get married, Hamilton. Have a family and that way you will never be alone. Family will take care of you when you grow old."

His words forever remained in my mind. He probably never knew how closely I paid attention. I never had the chance to tell him.

One night, I entered the break room to hear, "Surprise!" The nursing staff held a going away party for me. The room was decorated, and tables were lined with food and drinks. I noticed a money tree centered between everything. I was flabbergasted! My two years had come to an end, and I was leaving for Brazil.

"Wow," I said in amazement! Tears flowed, and I was touched by the generosity of my fellow workers.

I looked over at my partner, Mrs. Spikes. She was an older woman, and my mentor in some ways. Mrs. Spikes was my favorite. She taught me to be kind. She taught me how to show dignity and compassion to the elderly. She was strong and wise.

When I calculated the cash on the money tree, I counted $100.00. I was elated! That money would go far. Mrs. Spikes said to me, "You see Hamilton, it pays to be nice", and then she smiled her big pearl white smile.

CHAPTER 11

"*W*hat's that song?" I ask myself, "How does it go?" Oh yes; Peter, Paul, and Mary's version of "Leaving on a Jet Plane" echoed in my memory. Bags are packed and I'm ready to go.

The music of the 60s and 70s told a story about events we experienced. It was a pivotal time for the children of the era.

Malvina Reynolds, George Benson, Cat Stevens, Joni Mitchell, Peter Paul & Mary, Leon Russell, Joe Cocker, Yesterday & Today, The Cars, Marvin Gaye, Bill Withers, Tower of Power, and it goes on and on. Every song tells a story, and I felt as though each song was mine.

As I prepared to leave, Father and Mother help pack my suitcases for our drive to the airport. The weather was cold, but the air was crisp, and the sky was blue. We gathered up everything imaginable for my distant destination. My heart raced with excitement, and my mind continued to circle, racing from here to there.

"Do you have your passport and airline ticket, Tess?" my father asked. "Yes, Father, they are here in my purse," I said with a smile. Father returned to the car, warming up outside, and I took one last look around my bedroom.

I scanned the walls decorated with love posters of the 70s. I tapped the bobble head of Oakland A's team manager, Sal Bando, and silently whispered goodbye to my Rick Monday baseball bat. With great stature, the Oakland Raiders helmet rested on my nightstand. I ran my fingers across its smooth curvature. I leaned over and gently kissed the number 12. I exhaled and sighed at leaving it. I unplugged my mood lamp and noticed my alarm clock numbers flipped over to reveal 8:00 a.m. I reached down and opened a dresser drawer, pulling out the maroon sweater that Andre left for me. The distant smell of his cologne lingered on the sweater. I drew it close to my body and held it tightly. I then stuffed the sweater into my flight bag. Father honked the car horn, and I switched off my Clairol True-to-Light make-up mirror, closed my closet door, and slipped into my sheep-skin, leather coat.

The drive to the San Francisco International Airport felt like the longest drive of my life. Time ticked as I admired the San Francisco Bay beneath the San Mateo Bridge. The tide was high. The white caps rose and fell, while seagulls rested upon their backs. We had taken trips across this bridge before, transporting exchange students to and from this very airport. It was my turn. My throat tightened up.

Father helped with the checking in process. I lightly touched the fine leather on my luggage as it was transferred to a conveyor belt, and we briskly walked to my assigned gate. I felt tall in my platform shoes. I looked down at my mother, patting the top of her head. We both laughed. I locked arms with her as we took a seat at the gate. My mother's imagination regarding my journey turned her into a bundle of nerves. She stood and bounced from one foot to the other, babbling away, but all I heard was, "Wah-wah-wah." It was like the teacher in the Snoopy cartoons.

The airline announcement whisked me to my feet, and I stood as the airline personnel prepared the flight for boarding. It was time to say goodbye. We stood, embraced, and my mother said, "Be safe." With tears in his eyes, Father said, "I love you Tess; I am so proud of you."

I walked over to the ticket agent and handed her my boarding pass. I took another glance at my parents and waved goodbye.

"I love you," I said under my breath. Tears streamed down my overjoyed cheeks and rested upon my dimples.

It was March 5, 1974. I boarded the Pan American Boeing 747 aircraft. I sat back, made myself comfortable, and thought through my itinerary. My first stop would be the Los Angeles International Airport for one hour to pick up passengers. Afterwards, it would be a very long flight.

I removed the letters from Andre, and then I pushed my carryon bag under the seat in front of me. There must have been at least 20 of them. With uncertainty in my heart, and hope for a future, I read them, one by one, over and over.

CHAPTER 12

"*L*et me read it!" My mother shouted. The mail man had just delivered a special delivery letter. It was a letter from Andre.

Andre would write the most romantic letters. They were simply poetic. In my mind, they were as good as the love letters from the great romances of ancient history. After losing myself in his writings, I would share Andre's letters with my mother. She seemed to live vicariously through me. I imagined, for her, she missed out on the adventures I experienced. Mother was married and pregnant by the time she was twenty years old. She became a mother too soon and never lived on her own. My grandmother once told me, "Your mother was always pregnant." After seven pregnancies, I think she was accurate. Perhaps her fantasies were our unspoken love language. My mother admired me, yet she never told me. I wished I knew her inner feelings, her sorrows, and her triumphs.

The telephone rang, and mother announced that another phone call was for me. It was usually a girlfriend; I had many. We would talk about our plans for the weekend. There was always a party to attend, or a dance being held. It was the 70s after all, and I do not remember a dull moment.

My girlfriends and I loved to attend the Battle of the Bands. Local bands, or garage bands as I called them, assembled and competed against each other with their music talents. It was common to walk around my neighborhood and hear bands playing in their garage. The garage doors would open, and we would converge in the driveway to watch them play. Sometimes the bands rented a warehouse near the end of runway 10L, at Hayward airport. Friends and I would pile into my father's car and head over to their rehearsals.

Some musicians rehearsed in their apartment living rooms, and we hung out on their balcony, or in the kitchen. Little did I know, the foundation was being formed for the bands that would make history.

We would turn up at dances featured in high schools, junior high schools, grammar schools, and sometimes church community centers. With cigarettes in hand, we would make our entrance as the cool chicks. The guys would check out girls, and girls would check out guys. The bands were set up on stages, with hot ice vapors glowing through the soft mystic lights. The rhythm penetrated my body, starting at my feet and moving up to my shoulders. I grabbed the first available guy and danced.

The evenings usually ended with a cruise down East 14th street, called the strip. The street ran between Oakland, San Leandro, San Lorenzo, and Hayward. On Friday and Saturday nights, cars and trucks lined the strip, bumper to bumper. They drove down one side of the strip, made a U-turn, and then drove back the opposite direction. Other vehicles were parked along the edge of the street, and teenagers gathered around them or sat on their hoods.

It seemed harmless. Most the time we checked out the guys and honked. There were some moments when trouble would be made. My friends and I, were once chased by a car full of girls. I was in the back seat of Yvette's mustang. All my girlfriends were yelling, lots of hand gestures, and honking. It never amounted to much, but it made for an eventful evening.

In high school, we had the customary social groups. There were the raw-raws, or the politically correct term, cheerleaders. The studious friends were the nerds. The hard asses (not literal) were the troublemakers. And then there were us. I'm not sure what we were. I guess we were the soft asses, with a hard ass attitude; somewhere in the middle. I was an average student, but always had a compulsive drive.

I was the first woman accepted into the auto mechanics course. I loved working on cars and the mechanical challenge. Because the class required each student to pair up, the administration didn't think it would be appropriate for me to pair with a boy. It seemed that would be my plight in life. Judgement fell upon me, due to my mien. I dropped by my counselor's office to supplicate my case, and he insisted that I find a female student to enroll with me. Luckily, an under-classmate, Annette, overheard my dilemma and signed up.

My auto mechanics teacher, Mr. Abbotown, allowed me to work on my 1958 Volkswagen Karmann Ghia in the school shop. Sometimes after school, we would work together on more complicated repairs. My emergency brake cable had broken, and he offered to help me replace it. I can still see Mr. Abbotown lain underneath my car staring up at me. As I maneuvered the cable from the inside console, his brown eyes were peeking through his thick eyeglasses, a bit of oil was smudged on his nose.

We worked well together, and his patience and teaching principals were impeccable. In the event of any unexpected breakdowns, his goal was to prepare me, and not be intimidated by an automobile engine. Troubleshooting had become my focus. His message sunk deep into my foundation.

My final test, in order to pass his class, was to rebuild a 4-barrel carburetor. Afterwards, I test drove our Ford LTD around the campus football field. About half way around, the engine had shut down. I immediately jumped out and opened the hood. I noticed the throttle cable had loosened itself. I reconnected it, started up the car, and drove back. The entire class had assembled to watch, and I was received with a standing ovation. Mr. Abbotown was proud. The syllabus proved to be a true challenge, but both Annette and I managed to finish, and pass the class with *flying colors.*

I was startled by the announcement overhead; "Please fasten your seatbelts and prepare for take-off. We are expecting some slight turbulence."

I was used to these bumps in the sky. When I flew with Father, we would laugh and he would say, "It's just like a bumpy road."

I settled back into my seat and watched as we flew over the coastal waters of San Francisco. I was comfortable flying. "Flying," I reminisced, *"Flying Colors."*

CHAPTER 13

*T*he stop in Los Angeles was short, but meaningful. I sat waiting for the arrival of new passengers, and a Brazilian man was assigned a seat next to mine. He was older than me, probably in his late 30s or early 40s. He introduced himself as Luciano. Italian by birth, he resided in Sao Paulo, Brazil.

Luciano had soft red hair, with fair skin, and green eyes. He sported long sideburns and a mustache. Luciano was intrigued about the adventure that awaited me. I shared my anticipation of reuniting with Andre. Luciano was my wing-man during our long flight, and I soon appreciated the company.

At one point, he reached into his pocket and presented me with a sterling silver bracelet. Luciano wanted me to have it, to always remember him. Those Latin men. We talked about his trip to Rio de Janeiro and about his expected return trip to Sao Paulo. We enjoyed our in-flight lunch, and afterward I was comfortable enough to drift off to twilight. My oldest sister floated in and out of my consciousness.

Katrina, or Katie as we called her, was five years older than me. She was a very popular girl growing up. She had many friends and was regarded as the beauty in our family. She had long, straight blonde hair, and of course was taller than me. Katie was good at everything. She was smart and received excellent grades in school. Katie majored in business, and she competed in gymnastic events. I always looked up to her and admired her, but Katie got annoyed with me; especially if I followed her around too often. She always had a boyfriend, and I even remember her having two boyfriends at the same time. I had no idea how she kept track of Jay and Joe. My parents screwed up on occasion, and called them by the wrong name.

It was interesting to watch Katie maneuver in and out of relationships. During her senior year in high school, her third boyfriend Ace, was voted cutest smile. Together, the two were voted "The Look of Love." They did make a nice couple, and they seem to be joined at the hip throughout the year, until Katie became very ill.

Katie was taken to the hospital one night because she was vomiting uncontrollably. She remained in the hospital for two or three days. The doctors ran numerous tests and worked to get her vomiting under control.

When she returned home, Katie remained in bed for a few more days. My father repeatedly asked, "Are you pregnant?" Katie laid there staring at the ceiling, not breathing a word.

I walked into her room, leaned over the bed, and whispered, "Are you okay?" She asked me to sit on the bed beside her, and she shared her diagnosis with me. She demanded I keep the secret between her and I. Not even Mother and Father knew the results from her tests. As I listened, my heart cried out, "You are going to die?"

Katie spoke in hushed tones. I leaned in closer as the words flowed. Katie suffered from terminal cancer and was not going to live much longer.

My mind raced, and I thought of Donald in his bassinet. "What?" The mortuary flashed in my brain. Father's words lingered, "He will be sleeping a very long time." The reality of his appellation appeared more real now. Donald never did awaken.

I sobbed quietly on the bed beside my sister. I was only 12 years old, but I realized this meant a very long sleep was in stow for her.... a long one indeed.

~

I JARRED SUDDENLY WHEN THE CAPTAIN SPOKE OVER THE INTERCOM, "Please fasten your seatbelts and prepare for our descent into Panama City." I had been resting my head on Luciano's shoulder and bolted to an upright position.

It was still daylight when we were asked to exit the airplane, allowing for cleaning, and to pick up additional passengers. I looked at Luciano and laughed. "So sorry," I said. He smiled, "No problem." He had that Brazilian accent, reminding me of Andre.

The airport was packed with vendors of all sorts. There were young kids, old men, shoe shiners, and women selling varieties of flowers. I felt as though I had stepped back in time or arrived on another planet. People stared and rambled in foreign languages. Thanks to my seventh-grade Spanish class, I understood a few words. I smiled and continued walking about. It was noisy in the terminal. Dogs ran about barking, and I could smell the foul persistent odor of urine. People gathered around each gate, and I could have taken a walk outside, but did not dare. I preferred to stay close to my wing-man. He provided a sense of safety. I felt that I had known Luciano my entire life.

A foreign, scratchy voice came over the loudspeakers in the termi-nal. I could make out a few words, including what sounded like my flight number. I looked to Luciano for confirmation, and I was once again boarded in the comforts of the Pan American Airlines. I slipped back into my seat and flipped through some of my letters from Andre. The sound of the aircraft engines at altitude carried my thoughts away as Luciano rambled on, and on, about himself.

I wondered how Andre would react when I saw him again. I hoped he would be happy. I pushed my seat back into a reclined position. I closed my eyes, "Soon." I said to myself, "In a twinkling of an eye."

CHAPTER 14

"*H*ey, you want to skip class today?" Darcie was a Spanish girl with big brown eyes and dark brown hair. She was pretty and loved to live on the edge. We met in seventh grade and had been close friends ever since. It was our junior year of high school, and Darcie had a 1966 Chevrolet Corvair. Darcie dated a young man who enlisted in the US Army. He was stationed at Fort Ord in Monterey, California, and was graduating from basic training. Darcie wanted to attend the ceremonies, but her parents forbade her from going. She was determined to go regardless of orders from home.

I looked into Darcie's eyes. She was so persuasive. "Ok," I said, "Let's go."

We jumped into her Corvair and headed south on Highway 17, ditching school. I reached over and tuned in our favorite radio station, K.F.R.C.

It was a beautiful drive to Monterey and yet somewhat surreal. The coastal highway turned and followed the lovely eucalyptus trees. The air was heavy, and the smell of salt was pungent. I turned up the volume and tapped my feet to the rhythm of George Benson's "Body Talk." We both laughed at the thought of skipping school. I had never done that before, and I found it exhilarating.

We arrived at Fort Ord on time for the outdoor ceremony. The chairs were lined up for family and friends. A marching band made its way across the field. We sat before a platform of uniformed officers, and the commencement began. Darcie's boyfriend marched in with all the graduating companies. It was a moving ceremony, and there wasn't a dry eye in attendance. The soldiers tossed their hats in the air, and everyone cheered.

I was very proud of the graduates. They seemed so grown up to me. The men represented our country, and their sacrifice and devotion for my freedom had me thinking about the great commitment they made. I looked up and gazed at our nation's flag rippling in the wind.

For a brief moment I saw the flag on top of the Alameda County Courthouse. I notice the clouds forming in the distance and the blue sky. My smile faded. "Freedom," I whispered under my breath.

Darcie and I had said our goodbyes and jumped into her Corvair before heading back to San Leandro. It was getting late, and we needed to be home by 5:30. It was already nearing 2:00.

We traveled north on Highway 1 and transitioned over to Highway 17. As we approached the small town of Los Gatos, Darcie noticed black smoke coming out of the back of her car. We immediately pulled off the road. I opened the hood which was located in the back of this car and immediately realized the fan belt was gone. "Looks like the belt broke, and oil has spewed all over the engine," I said to Darcie. I knew we were *screwed*.

Darcie and I stared at one another in disbelief. It was a wonderful day, and abruptly we faced the problem of how we were going to get home?

As we stood along the side of the freeway, we noticed a Highway Patrol car edging near. We swayed back and forth as cars raced past us, one by one. The patrol car slowed to a stop. What luck for us. The patrol officer exited his car and began asking questions. We explained our situation, but I was afraid we would get in trouble since we were minors and not in school. The kind officer offered to drive us into town.

It was my first experience in the back of a Highway Patrol car. It felt unusual and a little uncomfortable. I kept looking out of the back window at the passing cars. I felt like a convict and wondered, "Is this how Father felt when he was arrested and taken to jail?"

We drove down the highway and into Los Gatos. The officer offered to get us to a service station. I think he knew the owners of the establishment, because it was closed and he managed to radio for help.

It was not long before two men arrived at the station. I looked over at Darcie and then back at the two men. "We do not have any money, and we cannot pay you. We are stranded, and we are penniless," I said with a nervous smile. My mind drifted to pennies landing on the ground, and then pennies landing on The Salvation Army drum.

The two men glanced at each other and then glanced back at us. I felt like they were sizing us up. They both insisted that it was okay. One of them unlocked the front door to the station; I assumed that he was the owner. Back then, gas stations were also repair facilities, and it did not take long to find the parts that were needed. All four of us loaded into a pickup truck, along with some automobile oil, and a fan belt. The bench seat reached across the older truck, requiring Darcie and I to squeeze in between the two maintenance men.

As we headed down Highway 17, the conversation between the four of us was minimal. Darcie and I were nervous and scared. It felt like forever when we finally spotted Darcie's car on the side of the freeway. The old truck made a sweeping turn around the off ramp. Strangely, the driver took the opportunity to lean over and open the glove box. I had no idea why he did that, but Darcie and I noticed a handgun in the glove box.

My stomach wrenched with feelings of disbelief. I had felt a numbing feeling move from the tips of my toes to the top of my head. I thought of Mr. Abbotown, my auto shop teacher, and knew he would be disappointed in me.

Darcie squeezed my leg- hard- and we glanced at each other. "Oh shit," I said to myself, "I think we are *screwed*, again."

CHAPTER 15

"*P*lease fasten your seatbelts and bring your seats to the upright position," the authoritative Captain broadcasted. I was awakened to find the passengers and crew preparing to land at our next destination, Lima, Peru.

It was dark. It was nearly midnight when I exited the aircraft. Luciano was by my side. I felt the heat hit my face. It must have been 100 degrees.

I was directed to change planes, and I had about an hour-long wait. The Sao Paulo-Guarulhos International Airport was not able to accommodate 747s. Those large jets had the potential to shatter windows upon arrivals and departures. I transferred into a smaller aircraft, a Boeing 707.

Luciano changed planes as well. Before parting, we exchanged phone numbers, and I watched my wing-man walk down the terminal hallway, disappearing into the lumbering crowds. I felt alone again; however, the thought of my last stop gave me joy.

I found Lima to be an interesting stop. Strangely there were many children about in the middle of the night, and I remember thinking "Why are they *not* in bed?" The dark-skinned kids sold all kinds of trinkets, including bracelets, watches, and beaded necklaces. The terminal was filled with vibrant colored flowers. The air was thin and the smell of perspiration resonated throughout.

There were a handful of boys that babbled in Spanish and wanted to shine my shoes. I gave in to one small boy and allowed him to polish mine. I took my seat, and he began working very hard at making my shoes sparkle. At times, he glanced up at me with his big brown eyes. The whites of his eyes were exceptionally white against his skin. We seemed to have our own special unspoken language; I couldn't help but smile. Children, in any part of the world, are so beautiful.

I felt a man staring at me. I wondered, "What is he thinking? Do I look lost?" The moment caused me to recall a dark memory when I was young. I was very young, and it was dark there too.

MY MATERNAL GRANDMOTHER, FLORA, WAS A HOUSEKEEPER/COOK, AND her husband, Ralph, was a caretaker. They resided at Laguna Seca Ranch, which sits east of Monterey, California, in Santa Clara County.

Whenever the owners of the house were out of town, my grandmother would invite us to stay at the ranch. The home was big and luxurious. I remember the home was built around their swimming pool and the rooms faced the pool. There was a lot of glass and no drapes or curtains. The property was well wooded, and privacy was not an issue.

It was a big beautiful place with tennis courts, shooting ranges, and a golf course. My brother, Albert, loved the horse stables most of all. They were racing horses that the family transported to the race-track. I was first introduced to a remote control in the house's movie theatre. The television screen transmitted black and white images, or perhaps my memory of this place is black and white. My brothers and sisters would fight over who could hold the remote. Most the time, my brothers won the battle.

Ralph would treat us very special. It was all a show, though; it was a show for my mother. My sisters and I would rush to the swimming pool almost as soon as we arrived. We would spend hours in the pool swimming and play pool games. My grandfather would join us, and because he was keeping an eye on us, my mother would retire to the house and visit with *her* mother.

He drove us around the ranch in their beach car. It was a Fiat 500 Ghia Jolly fitted with wicker seats. It was considered a luxury get-about-town car for the elite. Grandpa Ralph seemed to be a nice man, at least to the world outside of mine, he was.

The sun slowly set above the horizon and after a nice meal prepared by Grandmother, we would get ourselves ready for bed.

Late at night, Grandpa Ralph entered our room where my sisters and I slumbered. He came in very quietly and took *her*. I wasn't sure where they went, but I laid still and pretended to be asleep. I saw him half naked, he only wore his undershirt. I was frightened, and I became lifeless. She left quietly with him, and I did not make a sound. I wondered why *she* was taken. I did not understand. I should have screamed, yelled, and fought for my sister, but instead, I froze. I never wanted to be taken.

Step Grandfather Ralph passed away years later. I recalled the funeral service for him. Grandma Flora grieved over his body as he lay in his casket. My sisters and I stood beside her looking at him and then, there was that stern whisper in my ear, "I am glad he is dead... He can never touch me again." Grandma never knew, but we did. It was our secret.

This beautiful place was not the ticky-tacky home I felt safe in. No matter how much money you have, *it does not prevent darkness.*

SLOWLY, MY EYES BECAME FOCUSED. I CLEARLY SEE THE MAN'S GLARE AT this foreign airport in the heart of South America. He smiled, revealing his yellow teeth. I casually got up and paid the young boy for his hard work. I wanted nothing to do with the man who gazed upon me, especially here and so far from home. "I hope we board soon," my mind chanted. I missed my wing-man.

CHAPTER 16

 y sister, Angelina, was the bomb-shell of the family. She was the second oldest and my only sister who was a brunette. She reminded me of Cher. She was cool and very independent.

Angelina studied to become a hairdresser, or beautician as we referred to back then.

We called her Angie, her nickname. Angie did not see herself as beautiful, but she was. She was the most striking of us four girls. She had big blue eyes and was much taller than I was.

When Angie was attending seventh grade, a local high school student cast his eyes upon her. He would pass by our home on his way to school. It wasn't long before he made his move, and Mel became a household name. Mel was four years older than Angie. He grew up just down the street from us in the same ticky-tacky neighborhood.

Mel and Angie were always together. Mel was funny and looked just like Ringo Starr, without the drum set. They were my role models. In my eyes, they were the perfect couple.

When Angie and Mel married in 1973, I was asked, along with my other two sisters, to be in their wedding.

It was a beautiful wedding, in the traditional style beginning at our local church, and following at The Peralta House; downtown San Leandro. This was the first brick house built in Alameda County, in 1860. My sister selected the perfect venue. The entry was surrounded by gardens, with the sweet smell of gardenias. Water fountains flowed, and a fine mist of water cooled the air. All my aunts, uncles, and cousins attended, and most were from southern California.

My mother, and Grandma Flora, took on the heavy task of composing the menu. They prepared for days prior to the event. Mother not only cooked, she found time to design and sew all the bride maid gowns, as well as her own. I helped with the sewing, and between all of us, Angie's wedding day unfolded beautifully.

The wedding event concluded at dusk, and my cousins wanted to drive over to San Francisco.

A drive through the Height Ashbury district had become a popular visitor attraction. It was famous, and it was the 70s, and I was taken back by their request. I did not share in the glamour of this event, so I stayed behind while my older sisters, brothers, and cousins headed over to the city.

I was invited to an engagement party that night for Arthur and Louisa. I went to school with Louisa, but I had not met Arthur. I changed out of my gown into my party clothes. I wondered how my cousins and family were enjoying the city. I thought they were silly. Little did I know, history was being made right under my nose. Years later, the hippies who lined the streets of Height and Ashbury were infamous.

The phone rang, and I jumped to answer it. There was a voice on the other end, a voice I did not recognize. It was a man, and he said, "Is this Tess?" "Yes," I answered. As I listened, my mouth dropped open.

"ALL PASSENGERS PLEASE PREPARE BOARDING FLIGHT #177... TO SAO Paulo, Brazil." I proceeded to board and settle into another flight for my final leg to Brazil. "Six hours," I told myself. We departed from Lima, Peru, inbound to Sao Paulo-Guarulhos.

It was a quiet flight. There were very few passengers aboard, and I could stretch out across the three seats in my isle. The flight attendant told me to try to sleep as this was a six-hour flight and it would be early morning when I arrived. I took her advice and drifted off.... deep in thought.

I cleared my mind of this mysterious voice on the other end of the phone line. A phone line far from here.

Ah, I thought to myself as I focused on the bulkhead above. I took in a long breath and exhaled slowly.... Elio.

CHAPTER 17

*E*lio Lencioni was hands down, the most handsome man I had laid eyes on. My sister Angie and Elio worked together at the Provence Beauty Salon, downtown San Leandro. Elio was the hairdresser I could not stop looking at before the prom. He looked a great deal like the singer-songwriter Cat Stevens, only with cowboy boots. I was struck in the most unusual way.

Angie often needed a model for new products and hairstyles, so I would attend night classes at the salon, so she could practice on me. I preferred to watch Elio, and think dreamy thoughts of him as Angie worked on a new haircut, permanent eyelashes, or a new color. Whatever it was, I was there. I jumped at every opportunity to admire him, even if it meant at a distance.

He was so much older (sixteen years to be exact), and I felt like a child when I looked at him. I watched as he styled someone's hair. I noticed how he held the scissors in his right hand, with his small finger slightly up in the air. I noticed his stance in his boots. I noticed the freshly ironed shirt, and his dark slacks. I noticed his long sideburns, and his shaggy hair hanging just below his collar.

I listened to him talk in a soft tone. He had kind eyes, and occasionally he glanced in my direction, and I quickly looked down. I felt myself blush, and I turned my thoughts away.

Years later, as I drove through a parking lot in my Karmann Ghia, I ran into Elio. His black Porsche Carrera approached, and I slowed to say hello. He was just the same handsome man with a beautiful smile. I smiled at him, he said, "Wow, have you grown up!"

I liked his comment. I responded, "Yes, I have, and I am nearly 18-years-old now."

"Can I phone you, Tess?" he asked.

"I am working at the hospital. Phone me there!" I said with a really big smile.

Elio and I went on our first date, September 23, 1973. It was a football game held in Berkeley at the California Memorial Stadium. Elio had season tickets to the Oakland Raiders football events. I admired Ken Stabler, "the Snake", as he marveled the crowds. His infamous jersey number 12 was embossed on the helmet Elio purchased for me. They defeated the Miami Dolphins that day. It was our first of many games, and it was cool hanging out with him. We did not talk too much; he was tongue-tied around me, and I was quiet. It was a simple wink, or nod from Elio, that radiated a comforting consolation.

Elio introduced me to many new foods. We would drive into the city for dinner at Fisherman's Wharf. As I close my eyes, I can still hear the distant ships in the bay. The sparkle of a full moon over the water, and the mist from our breath.

I became a sponge, soaking up every new experience. He became my first at just about everything. It was with Elio that I consumed my first lobster dinner. He introduced me to Bill Withers' music. He was cautious and handled me with soft, delicate touches. It was the first relationship that I felt grown up in. I had the first of many long rides on the back of his Harley Davidson. I had my first Christmas shopping experience with a man who bought Estee Lauder perfume just for me, and I had my first cup of coffee during the wee hours of the morning.

Elio knew that when I turned 18, I was bound for Brazil. I did not keep that a secret from him. He never felt threatened by that, nor did he express feelings of jealousy. Elio even bought my first piece of luggage. It was brown leather with needlepoint trim. On my 18th birthday, Elio took me out for dinner and surprised me with my *bon voyage* luggage. I savored the moments with him and devoured each second.

There were moments of conflict within me. This was not in my plans. I would find myself torn between feelings for Elio, and past feelings for Andre. Elio was comforting to be around. I felt loved, though he never said he loved me. I had hoped he would say the words, but I hung onto Andre's promises. I was determined to go to Brazil and reunite with my Brazilian love. Andre wanted to marry me, but Elio introduced doubt.

I OPENED THE SHADE TO MY AIRLINE WINDOW AND PEERED AT THE MOON surrounded by the southern constellation. I recalled the shimmer of its light above the San Francisco Bay. I loved this moon, so big, round, and bright.

The long flight allowed me to reflect on the past I was flying away from. I closed my eyes, and I could see Elio's eyes. They were a dark chocolate brown. He had one very small mole under his left eye, and another mole under his right. They were perfectly centered, and the exact same size. I would *never* forget him, his smile, or his eyes. I closed the shade and as I let my breath out, I whispered, *"Elio."*

CHAPTER 18

*T*he flight attendant woke me, offering a hot, steamy wash cloth that I received with a smile. Morning broke, just like the song, and I sat up and raised the window shade. The clouds beneath me gave way to small breaks, allowing me to see below. I saw green, lots of lush green trees. It was beautiful, and I wondered if I was flying over the Amazon jungle? I wiped my face with the warm cloth, allowing the excitement to close in. I whispered, "Close, I am so close."

Did we really have a guardian angel? Is that angel sitting next to me as my plane makes a descent into Sao Paulo? Was Luciano my guardian angel?

I know God protected me one night around my 17th birthday. Andre was gone, I had not met Elio, and I met up with my girlfriends for an evening of innocent fun.

My Father's 1970 Chevrolet Impala was named The White Cloud by my sisters and friends. I guess it looked like a big cloud coming down the street and it was white.

It was a dark night when I jumped in The White Cloud and headed to our local gas station. I pulled alongside the gas pumps and rolled down my window. I instructed the gas station attendant to fill the tank. Sitting in a panel van next to me, sat a leering man. I ignored him. This was not uncommon, but I was not aware he was watching me so close.

As I departed the station, he swiftly pulled out in front of me. I turned on my right turn signal and he abruptly turned right as well. We continued driving down a deserted street that led to our local park. I was nearly panicked and wondered what he was up to?

Unexpectedly, he swerved and stopped at an angle directly in front of my car. I had to stop, or I would have collided with him. My foot hit the brakes, screeching loudly as my body jolted forward against the steering wheel.

He jumped out of his van and approached the passenger side of my vehicle. Before I could reach over and lock my door, he was sitting in my front seat.

"Shit," I said to myself. "Why didn't I lock all the doors at the gas station?"

"Do I know you? Have I seen you somewhere before?" he asked.

I shook my head and said, "I don't think so."

"I know," he continued, "I remember seeing you in the newspaper!"

"Yes, I was in the local newspapers when I won a beauty contest," I responded. His eyes seemed to scour our surroundings.

I was so terrified. "Please go," I begged him. "You are not supposed to be in my car."

His dark crusty lips twitched. His brown face was creased with deep lines beneath his eyes. His black hair was traced of white. He wore a white undershirt with one sleeve rolled up holding a pack of cigarettes. He slowly reached for me.

"Please don't," I whispered.

He paused. His eyes scanned my body, and then he looked into my frightened eyes. Our eyes locked. He slowly raised his arm, hesitated, and opened the car door. He glanced down one last time, closed the door and left.

I leaned over and locked the door. I backed my car up and drove around him as fast as I could. I glanced in the rear-view mirror and watched as his image faded into the darkness.

~

"PLEASE FASTEN YOUR SEATBELTS AND RETURN YOUR SEAT TO ITS upright position." I was getting used to hearing that announcement.

I reflected on God's blessings. I was raised a Christian, and I believed that God was there for me in so many crazy times in my life. "Yes, I do believe in guardian angels," I reassured myself.

I looked out my window, and all I could see were buildings. I had never seen so many buildings in all my life. In 1974, Sao Paulo was the third largest city in the world, and to see the sight from the sky was incredible. I gathered my belongings and prepared for landing. The pilot made his final approach onto runway 09L. The airplane flaps deployed as our rate of descent slowed. I took my usual position watching the wheels as we approached the ground, closer, closer and then, bam! We touched down.

I thought about Father and smiled to myself. "Good Landing Captain," I said.

It was 6:00 a.m. in Brazil as I made my way down the stairs. I looked around at the tarmac and the building ahead of me. I was processed through customs, where my luggage waited for inspection. No one seemed very interested in looking through my suitcases. In fact, they never even opened my bags.

After I finished and left the little room, my Brazilian family greeted me. Sofia waved alongside my new Brazilian father, Udo. Our smiles met, and I waved to them. I ran to Sofia, and we embraced. I was overwhelmed with excitement that I couldn't hold back my tears. "Hello," I said to her father. He replied, "Oy." (which means hello in Portuguese)

After a short trip, I arrived in my new home. It was a beautiful house with marble floors and a winding staircase. I was received by my new Brazilian mother, Jolanda. She seemed nervous around me. I thought she believed I was a wild American California girl. Not sure why she felt that way about me, but I learned in time to deal with it. I was introduced to three new sisters, in addition to Sofia. Their names were Mariana or Nê, Elena, and the youngest, Suelita.

Nê was the oldest and spoke perfect English. She was a student at the University of Sao Paulo along with Sofia. The household included two servants named Anna and Maria.

Life in Sao Paulo was unique. It didn't take long before I addressed my Brazilian parents as Mamai and Papai.

My surprise to Andre would have to wait. I decided to rest and contact him that evening. I was jet-lagged and excited all at once.

I climbed the marble stairs leading to my new bed, in my new room. I admired the French doors, which opened to a balcony above our open garden area. The temperature was mild and a slight breeze created a slow movement to the heavy drapery that framed the doors.

My breathing slowed to a rhythm in tempo with the chirping music of nearby birds. Their song became saturated by the sounds of horns honking, whistles blowing, and bustling streets.

Sleep took over, and I drifted off.

CHAPTER 19

The sound of automobiles honking their horns woke me from my slumber. South America was full of sounds that I had not heard before. People honked their horns a lot in Brazil. They drove with one hand on the horn, the other on the steering wheel. My Brazilian father drove that same way when he brought me to my new home from the airport. He approached vehicles from behind and honked his horn, signaling them to move aside. No one seemed to get angry; it was their way of life.

As the evening grew near, Sofia announced that dinner would be served soon and that I was to dress up for dinner. We dined in a formal dining room. A long, elegant, carved wooden table was surrounded by ten high-back chairs. Each wooden chair was upholstered in needlepoint tapestry fabric. A chandelier hung from the 14-foot ceiling, lined with gold leaf moldings. Papai sat on one end and Mamai on the other.

The dinner was prepared from scratch and included fresh fruits, vegetables, and meat. Mamai had a small bell by her plate, and whenever she needed anything, she rang the bell. The servant, Anna or Maria, entered the dining room and waited for their orders. I thought,

"Wow, just ring a bell and wah-la, service." The Jetson's cartoon series came to mind, and I grinned as I thought of Rosie, their maid. We sure did not have that kind of treatment in San Leandro. We would serve each other, and then we would take turns cleaning the kitchen.

After a wonderful dinner and dessert, we adjourned to the formal living room where a beautiful U-shaped couch was paired, with a large square coffee table. The table had small drawers around it that housed tobacco, pipes, lighters, and cigarettes. We enjoyed espresso coffee, and for those who smoked, we relished our after-dinner fix of nicotine. Papai introduced me to pipe smoking. I found it very enjoyable and relaxing.

That evening, Sofia finally made the phone call to Andre.

His phone rang and rang, and after an eternity, someone answered. Sofia was my voice, since I did not speak Portuguese. Sofia handed the phone off to me, and I waited until Andre came to the phone.

"Hello," I said, and Andre was quiet. "Hello, Andre. It is me."

After the awkward pause, Andre shouted with joy and laughter.

"I am here, Andre. I am here in Sao Paulo!"

Andre and I talked and decided he would come over in the morning. He would take me out for lunch, and I could not wait.

I was finally going to be reunited with my Andre. I was so excited and so exhausted. As I hung up the phone, I detected Mamai with a soon to be familiar frown and one eyebrow raised. I was in a new home with new customs.

When it was time for bed, I politely kissed each family member on the cheek and retired for the night. "Tomorrow is a big day and I need my rest," I told myself.

When morning arrived, the sound of my Brazilian sister, Elena, woke me from my deep sleep. She hung out of her second-story bedroom window, shouting, "Sorvete. Sorvete," which means ice cream in Portuguese.

Every day, a man rode his bicycle by our home with an icebox on the back loaded with ice cream. Elena got his attention and ran down the stairs and out the door to buy a fudgsicle. She was a funny, beautiful girl with blonde hair and big brown eyes. She did not speak any English, and I did not speak Portuguese, so we communicated using a lot of hand gestures.

It was my first full day in Sao Paulo, and I was primed to see Andre. I was nervous and hoped Andre would still feel the same for me. Two years had passed, and I wasn't naïve enough to understand that we both had changed. Hours had turned into minutes, and soon the doorbell rang. I ran to the front door, swung it opened, and there stood my Andre. I jumped into his arms.

I was elated and consumed with emotion. We held each other for the longest time until I felt the eyes of my entire new family. It was Saturday, and they were all home and hovered in the background watching. I laughed and answered their stares, "This is my Andre." They smiled.

Andre escorted me outside to his convertible sports car. He opened the passenger door, and I glanced at the emblem "Puma" positioned on the side of his vehicle. I settled into my seat and buckled up.

I gazed at the second story of my new home and waved a goodbye to the attentive Elena. We drove down the road and through the neighborhood, passing the ice-cream man on the bicycle. I noticed the guards with bicycles positioned on each street corner; whistles hanging from their necks. Andre pointed out the numerous areas and talked about his city. We drove for hours, talking and laughing. He was finally right next to me. It seemed like just yesterday we parted at the airport in San Francisco. Time stood still, and it felt unchanged. It was as it was supposed to be. We would be together forever.

We drove to a quaint Brazilian café. People were seated outside under awnings, watching cars and people pass by. It was near the end of Summer for Brazil; the weather was beautiful in March. I memorized Andre's lips as they moved while he spoke, and my head spun with possibilities for our future. I never wanted this moment to end. I listened to every word, but my mind would pester, "Does he still love me?"

I forgot about time. At the age of 18, I was old enough to drink alcohol here, so Andre ordered a bottle of wine for us. Evening closed in, and we decided to drive to Andre's home, so I could meet his family.

We left and headed to the outer limits of this massive city.

A small dirt road led to a beautiful homestead. We drove through gates, passing guards at each checkpoint, and soon we arrived at the entrance of his home.

A guard opened my door and escorted me out of the car. Andre took my hand and led me into his home.

The beautiful entry introduced a much more modern home than Sofia's. It was one story, but spacious, and laid out much like the home my grandpa-Ralph cared for, in Laguna Seca. The house encircled the swimming pool. There were many places to explore, including tennis courts. It was just like a movie, and not at all like the song my father sang. We were not in the ticky-tacky housing project I grew up in. This was similar to that dark place, but the dark didn't penetrate the light of Brazil, and of Andre. It was the twilight hour; the sunlight streamed down on us, and the energy was warm.

"Bonsoir," I heard as I entered the living room area. Andre's mother, Reeta, and his father, Vitor greeted me. Reeta spoke Portuguese with a French accent. Vitor spoke Portuguese with an Italian accent. They were a charming couple. I smiled and said, "Hello."

We kissed each other on the cheek, embraced, and sat down on a beige leather sofa. It seemed that all I could do was sit back and take in their conversation. I understood, nothing. I gazed at this family of many cultures that had come together and resided here.

The beautiful sounds of their conversation were interrupted by footsteps. We turned to welcome the rest of Andre's family. I was introduced to Andre's brothers: Bento, Diogo, and Pablo. More handsome Brazilian men. Diogo presented me to his wife, Diaga.

A formal dinner was planned on my behalf. I was taken aback by all the kindness.

My hands shook, my heart pounded, and I told myself to just

breathe. I could not speak. I did not want to. I was here and all those dreams that I had about this life were coming true. My eyes scanned the room, and I noticed the photographs lining the walls with family portraits. I noticed the magazines on the coffee table. I noticed the shoes on Reeta's feet. I notice how small her feet were and her small stature. I saw the gleam in Vitor's eyes as he listened to his wife ramble on and on in broken French and Portuguese. I blushed when I noticed Andre staring at me. I gave all my attention to this moment. My head spun, and the ringing in my ears grew louder. My palms were saturated in sweat. It was still warm when the night crept in.

The full moon shone in the night sky when Andre and I drove back to my new home. The thought of Andre leaving me for the night generated a deepening sadness. This was our full moon, and my first full Brazilian moon. I was an adult, and yet I felt like I was still in high school. I had to respect the household in which I lived and return home.

I sensed something else as we drove through the streets of Sao Paulo. I wasn't sure what that feeling was, but it loomed in the recesses of my mind. I looked around and payed close attention to the headlights of the oncoming cars. The lights seemed much softer than the headlights at home. The streets were busy, but the noise subdued.

We arrived at my home, and Andre walked me to the door. It was a good day. I looked into my Andre's eyes, and I waited. His lips parted and out came the words, "I am dating someone else," he said. My heart stopped beating, and I felt like dropping to my knees. Andre had met another and was in a relationship. I was in the bottom of a pit and Andre was peering over the side at me, failing to reach for me. The words repeated in my head. My heart was broken, yet I understood. I had taken a chance when I made this a surprise visit. I had also found someone.

"Let's stay in touch," he said. "I will call you Tess, I promise. You will always be my one true love," and then he turned and walked away.

I remained still, listening as he drove his Puma into the distance. While I stood numb, I imagined a black Porsche passing by. I leaned back against the front door, looked up at my beautiful full moon, and

I sobbed. There it was. This moon was not the California moon that I took comfort in. It was Brazilian, and that night it was undesirable.

The Southern Constellation was not the Northern Constellation, and I was reminded that I had soloed abroad; my ship had grounded, and I stood on the steps of a foreign country.

CHAPTER 20

$\mathcal{S}$un light found its way into my room and rested upon my eyes. My father's mouth whispered little boxes; boxes made of ticky-tacky.

I HAD SLEPT DEEP. IT WAS LATE IN THE MORNING, AND MY BRAZILIAN family returned to their normal daily lives. I was the house guest. I was alone in the mornings until the afternoon when Elena and Suelita returned from school. Nê and Sofia had shifted into a full day of classes at the University. Mamai and Papai left each day. Papai went to work, and Mamai? I am not sure where she disappeared to, but she was always busy.

I tipped-toed down the winding marble stairs to the kitchen nook. Maria brought me coffee, hot milk, and fruit. It was a pleasure to have such pampering. I was blessed to be here, yet I felt such sadness and disappointment.

I poured coffee into the hot cup of milk. I stared down at the brown liquid for a long while and thought, "I love this coffee." I could love the espresso with hot milk and a bit of honey. There was love in the espresso. "The family and home will be my new love, my new adventure. I will take on the challenge of learning a new language." I smiled and sipped a bit of coffee.

The telephone rang, and I was surprised to hear my Brazilian mother answer it. "Is it a phone call for me?" I wondered. I walked towards the phone, hopeful that it could it be Andre? Mamai announced the call was from Luciano. I paused to absorb her words. That was unexpected, and I was pleasantly surprised. Luciano and I agreed to have lunch together in the near future. As I hung up the phone, I smiled at Mamai. She frowned as usual.

I am here. Yes, I am here. It reminded me of a Cat Stevens song. Cat Stevens reminded me of Elio. A tear broke free and ran down my face. "Shake it off," I told myself. "Life goes on."

The sun shone through the breakfast nook window, while the light layer of stratus clouds faded in and out of the sky, casting soft shadows on the light blue table cloth. I ran my hand across the table, imagining that I touched the sky. I sipped my last bit of new-found passion and retired to my bedroom. I rummaged through my dresser drawer and retrieved my swim suit. I had a typical American two-piece suit in red, white and blue colors. My Brazilian sisters argued that it was too big for me; however, I had not yet grown accustomed to the idea of wearing a typical Brazilian two-piece suit called a Tanga. It covered, nothing.

I quietly explored the house, stopping to admire Mamai's antique furnishings and paintings, making my way to the backyard. A garden area with palm trees and luscious flowers staged the scene. I sat my small radio on a table next to a chase lounge and relaxed in the Brazilian sun light. Music faded in and out as Diana Ross and Marvin Gaye sang. The lyrics grow in and out in strength.

I closed my eyes and let the warmth stream down upon my skin, causing beads of sweat to run down my chest, and gently rest on my naval. I listened to birds sing in the trees and inhaled the fragrance from the blossoms. Horns in the distance sounded between Diana's words as she sang to Marvin, "My Mistake." My chest rose as their words sank deep into my soul. My brain ran back and forth, and I drifted in and out of awareness.

In the distance, I heard a soft whistle blowing. It sounded to be some sort of language. A second whistle answered from a further distance. The banter between whistles continued. I imagined guards on the street corners mounting their bicycles and riding about with whistles in their mouth. I pondered what they could be saying? I continued to listen to the whistles when Maria brought a tray with refreshments and smiled, speaking to me in Portuguese. I had no idea what she said, but I nodded my head and thanked her. I felt spoiled. I reclined, pondering how I managed to make it here, and grinned.

The radio reception tuned in and out and the song of Cat Stevens' "Father and Son" faintly played. "Perfect, just like my new family," I breathed. His words, his passion, and his eyes filled my senses.

I saw brown eyes, and green eyes, and then I saw the blue eyes belonging to my father.

He bounced me up and down on his knee. I laughed with each bounce, encouraged by his smile. He sang to me. He hugged me. He held my hand. I smiled when he told me, "I love you a bushel and a peck."

"How much is a bushel and a peck?" I asked.

"A lot," my father had said with a grin, showing his clenched teeth.

I HEARD A PHONE RINGING IN THE DISTANCE. I SANK BACK TO THE memory of my white phone ringing on my kitchen wall. I ran to answer it, and I heard a man ask if I am Tess Hamilton? "Yes," I responded. "I want to offer you a job, I noticed your photograph in the newspaper, and I think you are beautiful." My heart raced at the thought of working as a model? "What kind of job are you offering me?" I asked. The man's voice a mystery. "I would like you to be my mistress. I would buy you beautiful clothes, maybe a car, and I could buy you beautiful panties to wear." I hung up the phone. I was appalled by this phone call. I wondered who he was, and how he had found me.

I recalled the crusty man on the dark street, as I drove away in a panic. Then I recalled my neighbor with the two young boys. His eyes lingered on my entire being.

A faint whistle had blown, a phone rang, and I wondered who are the people on the other end? My mind raced back and forth from Portuguese to English.

I am far away from them now, and no one will harm me here. I think of Chaim Topol as Tevye in *Fiddler on the Roof*. I remembered the scene during their Sabbath prayer. The family gathered around their dinner table.

I remembered the opening night in San Francisco. Andre and I had tickets to see this movie with his American host family. We actually sat and watched it, without participating in a lip lock session. Just thinking about it brought a slight smile to my face.

The movies' song, the words, and their love. I transferred those feelings from Andre to this moment. It warmed my soul to think of my Brazilian family, and the Brazilian sun above.

CHAPTER 21

*T*he bird sang loudly as I walked over to the birdcage. The birds' song became softer while the street sounds became louder.

I was ten years old when I stayed with Aunt Sarah and Uncle Pete. They had a very old home in downtown Oakland. It had ten-foot ceilings, and a grand entrance. An antique oak entry hall tree, with a storage bench, and beveled mirror greeted visitors. There were two bedrooms divided by a bathroom. In the bathroom, there was an old claw-foot bathtub. My aunt and uncle took me in for a weekend here and there. I felt like a princess in their care.

They owned and operated a small café called Pete's Eat 'in Time. My uncle worked behind the long counter, lined with stools covered in red leather. A wooden roadrunner bird teeter tottered behind the counter, dipping its beak in a small glass of water. My aunt, dressed in her Sunday finest, and always with her string of pearls on, did all the cooking. The small kitchen was situated behind a side wall adjacent to the counter. She peered through a window, without glass, and hollered to my uncle, "Order up!"

I felt blessed to be there. I would anxiously attend to customers, wash dishes, and clear the counter. When I washed the countertop and stools, I peeked underneath. There must have been one hundred pieces of chewing gum stuck under there. I did not mind the work, because my reward would be a hamburger with cheese on it. Aunt Sarah cooked one just for me and served it in a small basket lined with paper.

On occasion, Uncle Pete would pull out his Bolex 16mm movie camera. It had a zoom lens. I would smile at the camera and pretend I was a famous tap dancer. He and my aunt would smile as I entertained them with my wishful talent.

At the end of a long day, we would walk across the street to their home. Uncle Pete would put all their money in a coffee can and hide it in the house. The warm welcoming sound from a small green bird heralded our return as we entered. I was allowed to open the cage and gently take the bird out. I held it on my finger. And then it would fly about the house, often landing on the crown molding that lined the eight-foot mark on the walls.

On one occasion, Aunt Sarah and I went shopping at Capwell/Sears department store. It was a 380,000-square foot build-ing, just around the corner from their home. As we walked through the departments, I stopped to admire a pair of navy-blue bellbottom pants. They were the hip hugger style, and I must have been drooling, because my aunt purchased the pants for me. I was so excited. I would have a pair of bell-bottoms! They were my very first pair, and I was so proud to have them. It was my first fashion statement, and I felt grown up when I wore them.

At bedtime, my aunt drew a bath. I would lay in the tub for as long as the water was hot. I watched as drops of water dripped one by one from the spigot. I knew in my heart, as I soaked in the warmth of the claw foot bath-tub, it was because of them I learned *right from wrong*. My step-grandfather Ralph had mistreated my sister and me.

I remembered Ralph's large hands, and how he had hurt me. Just like my big toe as I raised my foot and rested it in the bath-tub spigot. I waited just long enough for the water to back up, and then I released it. A gush of water shot out. He disgusted me, and I was relieved to be right where I was.

Aunt Sarah would turn the electric blanket on in the guest room and warm my bed. The full-size bed was as big as a king-size. I didn't have to share with my three sisters; I had this bed all to myself. When I snuggled into the warm covers, Aunt Sarah said a bedtime prayer with me. She and Uncle Pete were indeed my guardian angels.

It is strange how different places and people can be. Idaho and Laguna-Seca were so cold; Oakland so warm. At times I never wanted to return to my ticky-tacky neighborhood, not wanting visitors during the night.

I listened to the little green bird chirp from the crown molding. I watched my Uncle as he napped in his easy chair. His belly as large as a Thanksgiving turkey. It rose and fell with his soothing breath. My eyes follow the motion of his chest. He would never harm me, and although I was changing from childhood to becoming a teenager, they never regarded me as a problem. My Aunt and Uncle's love seeded gently in my strength. Strength that would not reveal itself until much later.

Chirp, chirp, the bird sang. Bam, bam, my foot riffed. Honk, honk, autos sounded, and then I heard a whistle blow.

CHAPTER 22

"*How* do I look?" I said as I turned around in my new gown. Papai and Mamai were taking all of us to attend my first horse race. It is a grand social event in Sao Paulo. The women dressed in long gowns and big hats, and the men wore suits. President Ernesto Geisel would be in attendance. He was the 29th President of Brazil, during their military government rule. It did not matter who was racing, it was the event that captured me.

We drove to the Jockey Club. The stadium was sectioned off for the rich and the poor. The rich were seated in the finer section with overhead coverage from the sun. The poor stood in the grandstands without any shade. Our family was sitting with the rich and we had reserved box seats.

Crowds waited in anticipation. A bell sounded, and a large shot rang out. Once the race began, all I could do was look at people. My family pointed out President Geisel and others that held political status. As my eyes moved back and forth, they kept resting on the impoverished section. I remembered living in the Oakland projects, the long trip on a bus to Idaho, and strangely I sat all dressed up. I was as poor as the people I gazed upon.

My thoughts faded from the clamor of the racehorses to the waters beneath the ship's bow. The prolonged blast of the ship's horn sounded in the harbor. I watched as the water swirled and changed from a dark green color to crystal blue. I marveled in the climate and listened in anticipation of the small island that lay ahead.

I was on an adventure, along with Sofia and my three new Brazilian girlfriends; Luiza, Maite, and Pietra. The intense sounds of samba music played from the stern. I embraced the drum sounds and reminisced about our travels upon arriving here. It was not, by any means, a luxurious one.

We traveled by bus from Sao Paulo to Bahia. We purchased our round-trip ticket for $20.00 each. It was so inexpensive we went for it. My friends all came from wealthy families, and this trip was our way of venturing out on our own.

We boarded the bus and found that all the passengers were less fortunate than us. The people must have spent most of their life's savings just to buy a bus ticket. Their economic status was of no consequence to me. I was not from a wealthy family. I relished these moments. I recalled the time I traveled to Idaho as a child. This time the trip was my idea. I was ecstatic with the thought of going north into the interior of Brazil.

I was the most obvious foreign person, in comparison to our driver, and all other passengers. I stood out like a white panther with light blue eyes. People stared at me, and I smiled back.

It was daylight when we left, and we travelled for two nights and three days by bus. Each stop we made became more and more remote. The conditions worsened. Our bus traveled on a two-lane highway that turned into a two-lane dirt road. I sat and stared out my window, observing the towns as they turned into villages. Villages turned into jungle, and jungle turned into night.

I observed the twinkle of firelight, as we drove deeper into the country. Families gathered around campfires, while their huts loomed in the background. I observed homes without windows, doorways without doors, and feet without shoes.

I pondered if I was really seeing what I gazed upon? Before our bus ride, I had only observed these things in a *National Geographic* magazine. I immediately recalled the time as a child when darkness huddled around me.

"HAMILTON," THE LOUDSPEAKER ANNOUNCED. WE SAT IN THE WAITING room, Mother and my brothers and sisters, waited patiently. I was five.

We had to wait in a small room at the Soledad State Prison until it was our turn to visit Father. We were locked inside with only *National Geographic* magazines to look at. I marveled at the photographs of the dark-skinned people from third world countries. The tribal people were beautifully painted in many colors and adorned with hairpieces and jewelry. "I could not touch these people; they were not real," I told myself.

In contrast, I looked at my brothers, my sisters, and my mother. Mother had her usual nylon stockings, high heels, and dress on.

Sharing our tight space, strangers sat about thumbing through *National Geographic*. I felt claustrophobic.

A loud clank could be heard on the locked door. I stood as a guard instructed us to follow him into a spacious room lined with vending machines and tables. My father stood in the middle of the room, and we ran and hugged him.

Father's eyes teared up when he saw us. I did not understand why. I was too young to comprehend his emotion. I was just so happy to see him. Then, as young children do, we ran around the room and looked for money in the vending machines. If we found some, we squealed and bought a candy bar.

My eyes warmed, and I slowly opened them to the sun rising in the distance. We came to a slow stop for our morning breakfast. When we exited the bus, I was surrounded by people begging for money. The people were ill. It was like nothing I had ever witnessed. The diseases were many, and some, I was sure, were fatal. My Brazilian friends did not want me to talk or engage with the people, but I could not resist. I took out what money I had in coins and gave it to them.

We all approached our stop for food. We hoped to use the restroom, and we were motioned to the back of a building. The restroom was a concrete wall with holes dug in the ground for toilets. Flies circled about, and the stench was overwhelming. I passed a woman selling squares of toilet paper. I shook my head politely and mouthed, "Nao obrigado."

I suddenly did not have to use the restroom, nor was I hungry. We all hoped the next stop would be better. Flies continued to swarm us. People stared as we walked back to the bus. I looked directly in their eyes, and I could feel their pain.

The squeak of the bus brakes brought us to our next stop. It was a small village with many small children running about.

I was greeted by a group of children, poking and prodding at me. I was obviously not a local, and they were enchanted. I was intrigued with them as well, watching as they played a game with a stick and an orange peel. It was a bit like ice hockey. While resting, I held a small boy on my lap. He said his name was Douglas. "How can that be?" I thought to myself. Here I was, in the heart of the Amazon, and this boy had an American name?

"Douglas," I whispered as I kissed his cheek. He was not very old. I guessed him to be four or five years of age. He was a delight as he sat on my lap and allowed me to take a photograph. My friend, Pietra, had a Pentax 35mm camera, and she took our pictures as we played and laughed.

I paid him in exchange for the opportunity to photograph him. He begged me to stay. Douglas clung to me as I tried to climb the stairs into our bus. He cried as I hugged him one last time. "Take me with you, don't leave me!" he begged. He reminded me of the time I pounded on the car window when Father taxied away in his plane.

It later occurred to me that Douglas and I conversed entirely in Portuguese. I was amazed with myself. I did not need translation. I never forgot the boy. Douglas warmed my heart. It was a *National Geographic* moment. But this time I could see, smell, and hold it. It was no longer just photographs in front of me. The people stood before me, and they were very real.

I continued to gaze out my window, as we traveled north to the coastal region of Salvador, Bahia. The air was warm as night closed around us. We passed towns with people gathered in town halls; halls that were lined with people eating and drinking. I observed heads turning in our direction as we passed by.

I wondered how they lived, how they survived. It seemed the closer we got to our destination, that the quality of life improved. I realized that our bus journey had allowed me to see some of the most remote parts of Brazil. I loved every minute of it. It was my own adventure. It was a negative forever embossed in my memory. Life is as real as the images we see, even in a *National Geographic* magazine.

Staring out of the bus window gave way to the eyes staring back at me. It was in the darkest of night that my eyes finally succumbed to sleep.

CHAPTER 23

The memory of Douglas along with the intensity of the sun moved my heart. My arrival in Salvador Bahia welcomed a sea of new culture. Itaparica Island opened its doors to reveal a beautiful day.

The ship arrived at a small dock. None of us had ever been here, and we were excited to explore the next café and laugh with new friends. We settled for a day on a private beach. We dropped our backpacks and got comfortable on the sand. The water was a sleepy blue, almost iridescent. I went for a swim.

As I waded out into the waters, I savored the warmth of the sea. I never could bring myself to even wade in the ocean. I am deathly afraid of sharks, but the view overtook my senses that day. I finally let go of my fears, and I swam.

It was heavenly, and I floated tenderly in the water. Suddenly, my friends called out to me. They wanted me to come in from the sea. I swam to shore, and I leisurely walked onto the sand towards them, squeezing water out of my long hair. They babbled in Portuguese, and it took a minute to understand what they were telling me. I quickly turned around to gaze at the ocean. I finally saw it. A school of porpoises on its way out to sea. "They can be aggressive," Sofia explained. I watched as they faded into the horizon, and I was relieved they were not sharking.

It was time to move on, so we gathered up our belongings, and hiked down the sands to an outdoor pub. Music grew louder as we approached, and I realized that I was very thirsty. There were many locals at the pub. We walked through the crowd of patrons, and I could not help noticing how my eyes locked with each person I passed. It felt as though everyone was staring at me. I became somewhat uncomfortable and asked Sofia if something was wrong with my face? "Your eyes are very blue today, Tess," Luiza responded. I felt like that white panther again.

We sat down at a small empty table to enjoy a cold beer. Many men made conversation with us, and I shared that I was from San Francisco. Everyone seemed to know where San Francisco was.

The day continued to warm, and the people did too. We spent hours talking, laughing, and sharing our life experiences as we continued our journey. The small streets in Itaparica were decorated with small cobblestones, and old buildings of ticky-tacky colors. I noticed the attention that Luiza would receive. She was fair, with green eyes, and strawberry blonde hair. Brazilian women are beautiful. They carry themselves with confidence and take pride in their appearance. I paid close attention to her mannerisms' and hoped that one day I could be close to that perfection.

The ship blasted three horns when we entered the port of Salvador. The music increased as we neared the fascinating town. Voices echoed over the water, and my heart raced in anticipation.

It was just as I imagined; it was a town full of history, culture, and music. It had a marketplace at the port of entry that accommodated many vendors selling all their goods.

We traveled up The Lacerda Elevator, which was erected between 1869 and 1873. It connected the lower and upper city. The elevator door unfolded and we walked through the historical center into the upper city. Our hotel, Hotel Chile, was located just down the street.

Our room housed three twin beds. I shared a room with Sofia and Luiza. Pietra and Maite shared another room. It was a lovely room with a balcony over-looking the street. The cost was $20.00 each for the entire week. We had one women's bathroom with one shower down the hall. There was a dining room for our morning breakfast.

We walked out onto our balcony and gazed down on the busy street. Night had fallen, and lots of men were walking about. They called out and made gestures. Sofia soon made the connection that we were right in the middle of a red-light district. Street balconies were filled with prostitutes, and there we were, hanging out on ours. We quickly returned into our room and closed the shudder doors to our balcony. That was the last time we looked out of our balcony at night. It explained why our hotel room was so cheap.

Our time in Bahia was filled with adventure and some mishaps. We visited Voodoo houses, and I had my fortune told by a large Bahiana woman, dressed in traditional clothing. She predicted I would become a famous movie star when I returned to the United States.

As we meandered through the cobblestone streets, I stopped and took a photo of a man walking while balancing a coffin on his head. I consumed a cookie named "Cocada" made with coconut and brown sugar; it was unforgettable.

The town had built 365 churches; one for each day of the year. Sao Francisco Church and convent were decorated with gilt woodwork and paintings. When standing in front of this church, a reminder of the Third Order of Saint Francis was prominent. We toured as many churches as possible; all lined with gold artifacts and antiquities.

The most memorable church was the Nosso Senhor do Bonfim. The 18th century structure was located on the top of a hill over-looking the sea. The bus ride up the hill involved a man that took frequent glances at me. I'll admit that I looked back at him. I looked into his brown eyes, noticed his dark brown hair, and admired his dark brown beard. I felt that I knew this man, but how? I had not seen him before. I moved my eyes slowly down, sizing him up. I sighted his leather sandals. I tried to imagine him wearing cowboy boots. The thought made me chuckle.

I was suddenly distracted by the abrupt stop of the bus. It was time to exit. I stood on the street corner; I watched as the bus drove away, and in the window, I gazed at the sandaled man. He never looked away from me until the bus was out of sight. I watched as the bus disappeared, and I thought of Elio. The man had the same features and was close to the same age as Elio. Oh, how I longed for him.

"Come on Tess, let's go," Sofia awakened me from my pining and pulled on my arm, ascending the stairs of Bonfim. My mind quickly shifted to the present.

We toured Nosso Senhor do Bonfim's rooms, and walls lined with photographs. The ceiling was packed with plastic arms, legs, and heads hanging about. Sofia explained that people came here to ask God to be healed. If they, or a loved one, was healed, they provide the church with a photograph, and a representative plastic part of their body that was healed. I stood in the center of the room admiring the symbolic power of prayer.

I knelt down and prayed in that moment. Maybe one day I would be able to send my mended broken heart to this church? I envisioned my heart dangling from its ceiling. A peculiar feeling warmed its way throughout my body.

One day I would be baptized. I felt its power as I stood. A strong connection to the Catholic Church, though I was raised a Salvationist, permeated the air. It was a faith I had no knowledge of, nor had I studied. I was moved, yet remained motionless.

For our last night in Salvador, we decided to venture to an outdoor samba hut for dinner and dance. We summoned a taxi, and when we arrived, the music was already loud and people were dancing. We were seated at a table and ordered our dinner of fish, salad, and the traditional rice and beans. The volume made it difficult to talk, so we ate and took in the sound of Brazil.

The night was hot and the familiar ocean fragrance reminded me of home. I missed my runs to the San Francisco Bay. I hadn't run in Brazil, but I was certainly doing my share of walking. I smiled just as a hand touched my shoulder. I looked up to see a very handsome Brazilian man. He grinned and asked me to dance. I took his hand and followed him to the dance floor.

He wrapped his arms around my waist, as I admired his beautiful dark skin and sandy blonde hair. His eyes were green, and he was very tall. I followed his lead as we danced the samba, carrying us back and forth. Each beat of the music brought us closer and closer together. He drew me in with each step. We moved as one, our breath got heavier and heavier. His mouth was so close to mine. When his lips brushed slightly across my cheek, he smiled and gently whispered in my ear. Portuguese was no longer foreign to me, and his words were clear, "I cannot pass one minute without you".

His name was Luis. We continued with our dancing, drinking, and conversing. I was so happy, but my Brazilian sister, Sofia, was not. She was worried about Luis getting too close to me. She remained guarded, as though she was hired to protect me. It was the wee hours of the morning when we all shared a taxicab back to Hotel Chile. As I exited the cab, Luis gave me a final hug good night. I stepped out onto the curb and watched as Luis and his friends drove away into the darkness of this infamous red-light district.

The next morning, I received a note (left at the hotel front desk), from my samba dancer. It was his phone number. Luis turned out to be a university professor, residing in a town south of Brazil, near Iguazu Falls. He asked that I contact him. As I read his letter, I realized it was the samba, the ocean, the culture, the embrace, the kiss, the liquor, and my youth that consumed me.

I wanted to believe it was Luis, but I knew in my heart the likely hood of seeing him again was next to impossible.

CHAPTER 24

"Come on Tess, don't just stand there!" My grandfather shouted at me as I stood knee deep in snow. The bitter cold day in Idaho was perfect for my sisters' ice skating, but I was too small to participate. I shivered in the frigid air and wanted to go home.

I longed for the smell of the ocean and the sound of my brothers and sisters fighting. I wanted the sound of my father's voice singing that familiar song. The cold, bitter environment froze me to the bone. I can't have what I want. The bitterness of Idaho made me stronger, but I still resented it. My grandfather took my hands and moved me about. He attempted to warm me, but the snow and company kept me chilled. I hated him, and I hated being the youngest and smallest. "Leave me," I whispered.

I tried to warm my brittle bitterness with memories of little boxes that all looked just the same.

"Come on Tess, don't just stand there!" Sofia hollered at me as we stood waiting for a bus in Bahia. It was time to return to Sao Paulo, and I zoned out as I attempted to memorize the beauty of this historic town. I marveled at the people and soaked in the warmth of the sun. I closed my eyes and rotated my face towards the sky. A light dust of snow became a soft mist of warm rain. Idaho remnants lingered.

We boarded the bus and took a seat behind the driver. I wanted the best view possible, and the trip home reminded me how fortunate I have been in my life. I smiled at the driver and settled into yet another journey. The bus engine rumbled, and the coast drifted further and further away, fading into a distant memory. We ventured into the heart of the Amazon, and I wondered, "Will I ever return?"

The bus horn blasted and woke me from my restless sleep. The driver maneuvered through the small villages along a dirt road at night. Sofia and Luiza were sleeping, but I was fitfully sleeping and miserable because of a blasted sun burn. My back side suffered the hot sun's wrath. Maite and Pietra had traveled home by air. They could not endure another bus trip.

It was difficult to sit, and so I stood up front and visit with the driver. He was pleasant, and since everyone was asleep, I thought I could keep him company. I could have used some company too. We talked about who I was, and where my travels had taken me. He had not met an American before, and he seemed pleased to chat, asking me questions about my home and life in the United States.

I could not help noticing a peculiarity, as we passed buses or trucks coming the opposite direction. Each time we approached an on-coming vehicle, the driver would turn his left signal on. The vehicle approaching us would turn on their left signal as well. I found this odd. I asked him why they did this? He explained that it drew an imaginary line between each of them. This provided the vehicles a visual reference, so as not to collide. It was required when driving at night.

I thought about home; this would have given people a fright. It made perfect sense here in the remotest part of Brazil. The driver had a great sense of humor. He told me that he was a bus driver by trade and came from a very poor family. He missed his wife and children, who resided in Sao Paulo. He drove the route regularly, and it provided a modest lifestyle.

We talked about the people in Bahia. I commented on the women, and how they were able to carry large bundles of laundry on top of their heads, as they made their way through the cobblestone streets. We spoke about the vendors selling incense and spices. Strolling through town was intoxicating. We chatted about the port of entry, and how it housed rows and rows of merchants, fresh fruits, and many textiles of color.

I spoke about a beautiful hotel on the coast, with a lovely garden of flowers in the entrance that I had toured. The stucco walls and rows of neatly placed stones beneath my feet were beautiful. The palm trees dropped coconuts here and there, teaching me to look up on occasion. It was not uncommon to see a monkey in the trees. I did not care for monkeys.

I realized we had been visiting the entire night when the sun peeked over the horizon, and the clouds appeared to dance. The easy conversation reminded me how much I loved the language of Brazil.

There was melody beneath its rhythm, and each word was a musical note. Being in Brazil was like going back in time. It was simple and yet moving ever so fast. I was living in a city larger than the San Francisco Bay Area, but the South American city was full of life, laughter, and music. Oh, the music. The Samba music; the music that captured my soul.

CHAPTER 25

"*L*ook everyone, look!"

Our front door slammed shut and in bounced my father with a letter in hand. My father's short story had been published and sold to the *Alfred Hitchcock Mystery Magazine*. It was featured in the spring edition, April 1966. I was excited for him. The smile on his face, the dimples in his cheeks, and the gleam in his eyes were exhilarating. "We are rich and famous!" I shouted back at my father. Father laughed, and I laughed with him, probably for different reasons.

Father's story was about a cabin on the Old Dump Road. It was a scary story filled with suspense, mystery, and intrigue. He had such an imagination. My father began writing as a child. He would sit by the light of a small candle and write on scraps of paper. My father never stopped writing; as an adult he would pound away on the manual typewriter's keyboard. He kept his writings in boxes in our garage. He once wrote a novel that the *world* would read. Perhaps a movie would be made. I think my father lived every waking moment in some novel in his imagination, chapter by chapter. The movie never happened, and the novels were never published, but my father was a visionary master and had an imagination of grandeur.

Father was not at all like my Brazilian father. Papai was a serious businessman. He smoked cigars, dressed in suits and ties, and played poker at the jockey country club in Sao Paulo. He could be funny and kind.

Papai lived in grandeur, and his visions were all about land. He was a real estate developer. He and his brother owned a business named Braga & Braga. They hosted cocktail parties each Friday evening to support land development. Occasionally, I would attend these parties. They invited the important business people in Sao Paulo. It revolved around the who's who, and I would mingle with Papai's clients.

"Look everyone, look," Papai exclaimed. He stood over the small-scale map of properties for sale; cigar between his teeth. Little houses were placed in such a way to entice the prospective buyers. There were pink ones, blue ones, green ones, and yellow ones. Ticky-tacky, ticky-tacky, tick-tock, tick-tock, and they all looked.... I let out a silent breath, "Oh my," I whispered, "I miss my father."

THE BUS DREW CLOSER TO THE OUTSKIRTS OF SAO PAULO. THE MEMORY of my father and thoughts of my Brazilian father consumed me. It was daylight, and our return trip from Bahia was a long and tiring one. The familiar horns honking, brakes screeching, along with the grinding of the bus driver shifting gears, brought a smile to my face. I had been chatting with this bus driver perfectly in Portuguese. I was delighted with the progress I had made. At times, I found myself thinking thoughts in Portuguese. Father would be proud, and soon I would be reunited with Papai and Mamai.

I held tightly to the handrail in the front driver section of the bus. I stood on the steps leading out of the bus, and swayed back and forth, as the bus maneuvered its way through the small streets of Sao Paulo.

Soon we rounded the last corner, and I saw the bus station ahead. I was thrilled to see Papai standing outside waiting for our return. His big smile switched to shock when he saw me standing in the front of the bus. Evidently, that was not a position of high society. He reiterated my status here.

Sofia and Luiza gathered up our belongings, and we exited the bus. We had been away for ten days, and it passed so fast.

We settled into our daily routine once we were home again. A daily routine that was anything but routine for me.

"I could be Miss Brazil if I wanted to," Sofia said while standing in front of our full-length mirror. She was right, she was a beautiful young lady. She walked back and forth in our bedroom we shared, practicing her walk on the red carpet. I applauded as she did her quarter turns. All my Brazilian sisters loved to wear the latest fashions.

Sofia and I would grab a taxi, and shop on the famous Rua Augusta in Sao Paulo. We would walk the avenue window shopping, stopping to try on clothes, shoes and whatever was our fancy. I would make a point to patronize the bookstore, which housed many books in English.

Sofia also had her own seamstress. It was an interesting process, and nothing like I had ever experienced in the States. We bought fabric with our Brazilian mother, Jolanda, at a very large warehouse that hosted designers. A man would draw a design as you described your idea. He would then hand you the paper with the drawing, and this would be taken, along with your fabric, to the seamstress. The seamstress took measurements of your body. She would discuss your idea with you and then call when the creation was ready, or if any additional fitting would be necessary. At the end of the ordeal, a custom-tailored dress, slacks, blouse, suit or even a sweater was personalized and made specific for you. It was fantastic.

For the first time since I had arrived, I felt at home. I was surrounded with people who loved me. I lived with a family that opened their doors, their windows, and their rooms, and they *never hinted at darkness.*

CHAPTER 26

*I*t was a crisp summer morning in 1967, and I was startled by the sound of a horn honking outside.

It was Captain Hood from our local Salvation Army Corps picking my sisters and me up for a summer camp adventure. We attended the Salvation Army music camp nestled in the mountains near Santa Cruz, California. I was finally old enough to attend, and I was excited to attend camp for the first time.

We all packed ourselves into the station wagon, and I slid in front, right next to Captain Hood. He was a jolly man, and always full of laughter and promise. We traveled south on the Nimitz Highway to Santa Cruz.

Captain Hood was not only a rather big fellow, he was also a lead-footed officer. I remember the speed odometer would read over 100 miles per hour! I was not sure if we were running late, or if Captain Hood was just a fast driver. In any event, we arrived at Camp Redwood Glen, safe, expedient, and exhilarated to be here.

I was assigned to a cabin with other girls my age. I had a lower bunk bed, and I settled in with my sleeping bag.

We began each day with the sound of the trumpet playing "Reveille." We gathered at the camp flag pole and stood at attention.

We saluted the flag and recited the "Pledge of Allegiance" to The United States of America, followed by a prayer to our Heavenly Father. We then had breakfast in the cafeteria. We waited for our food together and always began eating at the same time. We learned respect for each other and how to work together as a team. Mail call followed our meals, and I was delighted if I was called up to receive a letter! Sometimes Mother or Father would write to me. It was nice to be missed, and old enough to know.

My oldest sister, Katie, was by far the most popular at camp. It was her first year as an official camp counselor. She was so pretty with her long blonde hair and beautiful blue eyes. She was seen walking about with this boy, or that boy. She bounced from one boyfriend to another, and there were times I was not sure who was the current love of her life?

I remember one boy that I thought was so sweet. His name was Fred Abrams. He was the best trumpet player at band camp. We had been sectioned off by our ability to play a musical instrument. Since the Salvation Army is primarily made up of brass instruments, I had to learn how to play one of them.

I chose the French cornet, which is a bit different from the trumpet. I was also assigned to the D band. The best students were in A, second best in B, third in C, and the worst in D. Need I say more? I did not mind, and I worked very hard to learn. I also had music theory classes where I learned to read and write music. I loved it here and learning to read music was helpful in my later years.

The free time we had each day was my favorite. I would swim at the built-in swimming pool. I would spend hours swimming and basking in the sun. I would watch the boys dive off the diving boards. They would compete and see who could make the smallest splash. We had a swimming event on Saturday. The older boys signed up, and would swim the length and back of the pool, underwater, without breaking the water surface. Fred Abrams and a boy named Jay Renquest swam the length and back, and the length again without coming up for air, or breaking the water surface. It was Jay who won this event. He also became my sister's next boyfriend. This entire camp experience was all about competing.

I became friends with Fred Abrams. He would fancy my older sisters, but was kind to me as well. I looked up to him. He was good at just about everything! He lived in San Francisco and his parents were retired from the Salvation Army. Fred later became a very famous trumpet player with a group called Tower of Power.

At bed time, we gathered outside the cafeteria for hot cocoa with marshmallows. It was a good way to end the day before jumping into that cold sleeping bag on my bunk. I remember getting into bed and pulling the bag over my head. My breath would warm me, and I would shiver until the warmth overcame the cold. The sound of "Taps" played in the background.

Sunday was our day of rest, and we gathered in the church for fellowship. I sat in the D band section when the music would begin. We played our best, and the congregation would listen. Many camp counselors, cooks, housekeeping, and clergy personnel were in attendance. Sometimes the faces on our congregation were all we needed to know just how bad our D band sounded.

The camp lasted for two weeks. We hiked, acted out plays in the outdoor amphitheater, played pranks with our neighbor cabins of girls, and enjoyed a bit of fun each morning when someone's undergarment would show up on the flagpole.

I noticed a young man who seemed to notice me each morning, and again in the afternoon at the swimming pool. It was a warm afternoon when he finally approached me. I was lying on my towel alongside the pool, basking in the sun. He stood over me and said "hello, I'm Charlie." I covered the sunlight with my hand, which made his face a silhouette. I sat up and smiled. "I'm Tess, hello Charlie." "I know who you are Tess, you are Katie's sister," he commented.

Charlie and I began our youthful relationship. Charlie was a few years older than me. He was taller, blonde and had blue eyes. His nose was a bit large, but his smile was all I noticed. We began hiking and exploring. Charlie wanted to hold my hand. This was new to me, and holding his hand somehow made me feel grown up.

We hiked deep into the woods one day, during our pool break. We found a fallen redwood and sat to enjoy the quiet of the sequoias. Charlie leaned in and made his move. It was my first kiss and evidently my most awkward kiss. Charlie's nose smacked mine, and I had no idea what I was doing. He began to explain 'French' kissing to me and so it was then, that I opened my mouth very slightly and allowed this young man to explore mine. Our front teeth collided. I was embarrassed, and I felt myself blush.

It became obvious that Charlie gave up on me. We stood and made our way back to camp. He did not hold my hand, and I began to withdraw. A few days later, other boys began teasing me about it. Hurtful words were said. Fred Abrams told me that rumors had it; I did not know how to kiss. He told me not to let those boys hurt my feelings, but they did. I began to mistrust boys, because that is what Charlie was; a boy. I felt used, humiliated, and betrayed.

Our final day arrived and parents came in carloads to pick up the campers. The finale took place in the church with a grand performance of musicians. I could see Father and Mother seated in the audience along with my new friends and families. One by one, students were called up front to receive an award. The camp recognized the best of the best. I sat patiently as names were announced and awards received, and then I heard my name. It was strange to hear my name in this large church and so unexpected since I was in the D band. I rose to this occasion, and it was announced that I received an "Outstanding Appreciation of Effort" award. My teacher felt I had gone above and beyond what was expected of me. I received a scholarship for the next camp season. My parents were very proud of me. I was very happy to please them, especially since I was not able to please Charlie.

The Salvation Army has always been regarded as an organization for those in need. Very few people regard this institution as a church. The church became a weekly part of my life until I became old enough to choose. In many ways, my family was of poverty. However, I did not see us as such. At camp, all in attendance looked the same. And perhaps we were.

The church was generous to my family. They sponsored us each year to attend camp. I did not realize it at the time, but came to understand later in my life. Without their support, I would not have had this experience; good or bad. The camp taught me practical life structure and the power of prayer. I learned to work hard. I learned how to lose with dignity and how to win with grace. I never did master the French cornet, but this did give me the opportunity to learn music.

I remained in D band year after year while attending camp. I should have played the drums. Drums pounded in my mind and yet, as I grew older, my eyes preferred the view at the swimming pool. The boys grew into young men, except for Charlie, and I into a young lady.

I may have been a slow learner, but eventually, I did master the art of French kissing.

CHAPTER 27

It was your typical evening in Brazil. Sofia and I attended a party, one of many. I noticed a Brazilian/French gentleman peering at me from across the room. We were on the 16th floor of a luxurious apartment. Sofia had motioned him over. His name was Noel.

Noel was funny, charming, nice looking, and carried himself with extreme confidence. He seemed to undress me with his eyes and unravel me with his lips. I was nervous around Noel. I tried to talk with him, but I felt he wanted to seduce me. For some reason, I had to prove myself stronger than him, stronger than any man.

"Don't touch me!" I said. The words flew out of my mouth, and I had no idea where that came from. Noel just smirked at me and walked away. I left the party that night without a prospective date, but deep down I knew why. My aura had evolved into a giant bubble that encased me. I was afraid to love and be loved.

A few weeks later, Mamai and Papai introduced me to Aberto. Aberto would stop by our home to visit my family. We shared quick glances at each other, and I sensed an attraction. He, being the family dentist, and single, was a perfect match for me, according to the family. I was still somewhat leery to date, but agreed to an evening out with him.

I was nervous when seated next to Aberto. He brought me to a beautiful samba house in downtown Sao Paulo. The samba music was loud and our table for two, was nestled in a small corner of the restaurant. The meal was superb and the company, delightful. "Call me Berto," he shouted over the music. Berto was handsome and nicely dressed.

He took my hand and led me to the dance floor. Very few words were exchanged between us. His motions were sensual and his rhythm perfect. I lost myself in that moment, and when I closed my eyes, I fought the urge to see otherwise. I wanted to be strong, stronger than him.

As the evening progressed, I became very comfortable speaking Portuguese, and Berto was uncomfortable speaking English. He was relieved when I voiced my preference to converse in his native language.

He appeared to be a gentleman who respected me, but he was very shy. I suspected my aura had grown in size. He seemed to be beyond my reach.

Berto invited me for a weekend at his family ranch. It was located in a small town, outside of Sao Paulo. I glanced at Berto, in his blue jeans and polo shirt, while traveling beside him in his Mercedes Benz. I enjoyed seeing him in a much more casual attire. It was a beautiful curvy road with rolling hills, ponds, and numerous roundabouts. The afternoon sun blazed in the distance. When we arrived, we were greeted by his friends, along with horse trailers and numerous vehicles parked about.

Berto escorted me into a lovely ranch style home. I admired numerous bedrooms, a game room, a large dining room and kitchen. Much staff personnel awaited our entrance into the formal living room. Berto showed me to a beautiful guest room that I would stay in. "This will be your room," he said. Again, another act from a true gentleman.

We gathered into the dining room for a nice dinner, and then to the smoking room for our after-dinner nicotine and caffeine. A tradition I became very comfortable with.

Berto and I walked the grounds and enjoyed a romantic sunset. Berto was planning a game of poker with his guests. I didn't know anything about poker, so I declined to participate. "Have fun," I said. "I will retire for the night." I was drawn to him, but as he walked me to my room, I wondered if we would only remain friends.

Berto drew me in close and softly kissed my cheek. "Good night," he whispered. I retired in my room, and nestled in the comforts of a full bed with feathered pillows. Elios' shadow reminded me, in his soft enduring way, how it felt to be wanted. I longed for his touch and in many ways Berto reminded me of him. Yet, with Berto he treated me as though I was a figurine to set upon his table. I was there to gaze upon and dust off here and there. Elio wanted to consume me. My mind pondering at this as sleep set in.

Cat Stevens' song "Morning has Broken" played softly on the radio next to the bed. I opened my eyes, smelled the coffee brewing, and heard voices about. I met Berto in the dining room, and we enjoyed our Brazilian breakfast. "Are you up for a ride?" he asked. Berto had a passion for horses, and the day's plan was for me to be a spectator of his equestrian talents. Berto and his guests gathered for a game of polo.

I perched myself on the balcony overlooking the impressive event. I wore a large brim hat and had my camera in hand. I waved to Berto as he galloped off with friends, dressed for the game. The grass field was in full view for my first exposure to polo. It was fun to watch as these handsome, skillful men blazed back and forth across the field. Servants attended to my needs of thirst, as I listened to the sounds of sticks slashing about and horse's snouts inhaling and exhaling.

I heard a bird overhead, and I thought, "I must praise God for this morning." I thanked Cat Stevens for the words of my prayer. I offered praise for the new day. The game was exhilarating, and I snapped as many photographs as possible. The sound of the shutter rhymes with the songs of the birds.

We settled into a quiet afternoon by the pool. The men were tired, and as I watched the sun setting behind the distant hills, women bathe in the sun. It was a picture-perfect day. I was miles from the small villages in the heart of Brazil. I had seen the poorest of poor, and today I socialized with the richest of rich. That was how Brazil was in the 70s. There were rich and there were poor, and not much in between. Where did I fit in? I was the in-between. There was light, and there was dark. I traveled to both sides from childhood to adulthood. From the rich with darkness, and from the poor with light. With Berto, I was with the rich with light, and only light. I glowed at this realization, as gratification set in.

I CLOSED MY EYES AND SOAKED UP THE SUN AS MY MIND DRIFTED TO THE memory of my sister Katie. I thought about how naïve I was. I believed my sister was going to pass away. I ran over to my neighbor's home the night Katie told me her terrible secret. Yvette was a good friend. She and I talked about Katie's cancer, and impending death, and we both had a good cry.

It became very clear over the next few months that my sister had lied to me. She was not going to die. She was pregnant, and I was a fool! When I confronted her, she just laughed at me? "What a cruel joke!" I hollered at her. The typical older sister. She shrugged and gave me *the look*. She always had a way of looking at me. She cocked her head to one side, raised the corner of her upper lip, and gave me the once over with her eyes.

I realized my sister was probably very frightened in her situation. After all, she was only 17 years old, and just a child at heart. Katie entered motherhood and had not lived her youth. Being the younger sibling, I was subject to her declination.

FAR AWAY FROM MY FAMILY AND MY SIBLINGS, I ENTERED A NEW WORLD, a new equator, a new star system, and yet the moon remained the same. There is only one moon, no matter where you run to or hide from; by celestial standards, that is. As the moon waxes and wanes, I would look at waxing as Elio, and waning as Andre, and Berto? He was seated on the crescent moon.

Berto and I traveled back to Sao Paulo. He eventually faded into a distant memory. He was probably enchanted with another. I began planning my next big trip to Bogota, Colombia. I was scheduled to leave Brazil soon, to visit my foreign exchange sister Luna. I had been in Brazil for six months. I looked forward to a new adventure, seeing Luna, and meeting her family.

Berto winked at me as he drove with one hand on the steering wheel, the other on my hand. We both looked forward toward the road we were traveling on.

Neither of us ever looked back.

CHAPTER 28

The ringing of the phone and the sound of my Brazilian sister, Elena, hollering my name, brought me down the winding marble stairs. I had a phone call from America, and it was Elio. "Elio Lencioni," Elena yelled. I was so happy to hear his voice. The connection was not great, and we both shouted over the phone to be heard. "I miss you," Elio said to me. This was music to my ears.

"I will return home in a few months," I told him. There was this echo that made it difficult to know when to speak and when to listen. We talked about my time in Brazil and how life was in the states. We only spoke for a few minutes. Long-distance phone calls were extremely expensive.

"I heard a song and thought of you," said Elio. "I was listening to 'Ain't no Sunshine' by Bill Withers."

I was filled with a warmth that came over me as I hung up the phone, and I turned to see my Brazilian family gathered nearby. They were entranced, hearing me ramble on and on in English. I was fluent in Portuguese, and English had not been spoken much in our household.

The next morning, I sat at my writing desk in my room, and composed a letter to Elio. I thanked him for the phone call and expressed my sincerest wishes to see him soon. As I sat writing, I looked up at the intercom on the wall and pressed the buzzer. "Yes, how can I help you?" answered the voice through this wonderful invention.

"I would like a coffee please," I said. As I continued writing, Maria arrived with a silver tray displaying coffee, milk, sugar, cheese, and bread. I thanked her. I sat back and realized; I had become comfortable in this lifestyle. I would leave in a few weeks, and the service would be missed. "Have I become a snob?" I thought. I shook my head and chuckled and continued writing.

I wrote in detail about the wedding of my Brazilian sister Nê to Paco. Nê was married the past month, and the wedding event took place at the Catholic church near our home.

Their ceremony was different from our traditional ones in the states. The wedding party consisted of the entire family. The father, mother, sisters, and brothers all stood in the front of the church. The bride's family lined up on one side and the groom's family on the other, forming a half circle. The priest stood center stage as Paco and Nê walked hand-in-hand down the aisle. Music played in the background, and we all rose for the occasion.

Nê was stunning in her wedding gown made from yards of silk. Her blonde hair and delicate hands complimented her beautiful eyes that sparkled when she smiled. Paco walked proudly next to her with an ear-to-ear grin. After a full mass, the priest announced Paco and Nê were man and wife. They embraced, kissed, and received blessings from her parents and then from his. The entire family united and followed Paco and Nê out of the church.

Afterward, we gathered at our home for the reception. I was amazed how the home was transformed into a beautiful venue. Our patio was draped with awnings, furniture was removed from different rooms, and bedrooms housed long tables displaying wedding gifts that had arrived days before the event. Guests wandered about admiring the gifts, food, and whiskey. Yes, whiskey was the drink of choice. Whiskey over ice, and I never did acquire a taste for it.

I folded my letter, and as I slid it into the envelope and sealed it, I intentionally left out the part about being introduced to Berto. I recalled saying hello to him, and I recalled when I looked up into the sky, I saw the crescent moon.

How is it possible that I could long for the ticky-tacky life back in the states when I was surrounded by love, safety, and beauty? It was the grandeur that my father dreamed about. It was the grandeur that I thought about when I watched airplanes land at the Oakland airport. It was what we enjoyed in Sao Paulo, Brazil. My heart was torn, but I knew it was only a matter of time that I would be returning to the ticky-tacky neighborhood; called home.

CHAPTER 29

$\mathcal{L}$eaving on a Jet Plane. Peter, Paul, and Mary's song poured from my mind

~

I PACKED SIX MONTHS INTO MY SUITCASES, AND THEY WERE LINED UP just inside the entry to my Brazilian home. I made my way to the formal dining room for our last dinner together. Mamai planned my favorite foods for my last dinner. Maria, the cook, was sad. We had become friends, and I considered her family. She had prepared a wonderful dinner of steak, feijoada (Brazilian black beans and rice), salads, vegetables, breads, and sauces. The dessert was a pineapple cake with a coconut icing. It was to die for. After dinner, we retired to the smoking room for our last communion of nicotine and coffee.

My Brazilian family drove me to the airport that night. I had a midnight flight out of Sao Paulo. My itinerary included a stop in Caracas, Venezuela, and from there another flight into Bogota, Colombia. Mamai babbled away about how she was going to diet after my departure. She went on and on, about this and that, before abruptly turning to me in the back seat. She asked if I understood what she was saying? "Yes," I responded in Portuguese, and I paraphrased my interpretation. Amazed, she exclaimed that I had indeed learned and understood Portuguese. I felt triumphant and pleased with myself. She didn't frown.

As we sat in the airport, waiting for my flight departure announcement, I heard a familiar voice. I was surprised to see Andre running into the terminal gate. He had brought Sonja Santos with him. They decided to drive to the airport and see me off. I embraced Andre and Sonja and exchanged our good byes. I was so moved that I began to sob, not sure if my tears were of joy or sorrow.

Our lives together began in my home of California, and ended in theirs, Brazil. It was me that was leaving this time, and there was no promise of seeing them again. I had braided them inside my heart, and every strand of hair was an emotion. I was loved and loved them, yet I was leaving. I prayed that the weave was tight, and I would never lose them.

I waved my goodbye, just as I did my father and mother in California, only this time, I waved to my Papai and Mamai, my sisters, and my friends. My family had grown and so had I.

I settled into my assigned seat on the Pan American 707 and looked out the window. I waved once more. I could not control the tears, and I had not cried like this since Andre left me at the airport in San Francisco. I could still see his plane departing. Sofia stood beside me, holding me close as he waved goodbye. She knew my pain and my heart break.

Tonight, I saw beyond Andre, and the sound of his Puma driving off in the distance. I was leaving him, however this time, the hope of seeing him again was mislaid.

"Fasten your seat belts," the command broke my train of thought. I buckled in and sat back as the captain rolled out on to runway 09L. The exhilaration and sound of the jet engines reminded me of my father. I waited for the rotation and smiled as we ascended into the sky. I wondered what was next. And who will I meet? My breath was shallow as I continued to look out the window. It filled with darkness, and then the twinkling of stars. As the sky gave way to the light of the moon, I had noticed it was waning.

"The moon," I said to myself as I closed my eyes.

CHAPTER 30

"*W*ake up, my darling," Elio whispered in my ear. I peeked at Elio's brown eyes, reflecting the soft smile placed on his lips. I felt the warmth of his touch and strangely heard some lumbering sounds around me. I squeezed my eyes shut, and again I felt his touch and turned to get up. I opened my eyelids, and the flight attendant handed me a warm cloth. It was still dark, but she whispered, "We are about to arrive in Caracas." The sun had not risen, and as the fog lifted from my mind, it was clear that I was far away from Elio.

Our flight crew offered me a cup of coffee. As I sipped the coffee and warmed my face, I thought of Sonja Santos.

Sonja and I met in San Leandro when she lived with the Tupper family next door. Sonja arrived from Sao Paulo, Brazil, in 1973. It was the same year as our own foreign exchange sister, Luna. She and Luna became friends. Sonja and Andre had a history together. They shared the same friends in Brazil. We had a great time in America while she was there. Lucky for me I was able to spend a few days in her home while in Brazil.

Sonja lived with her mother and younger brother. She was zealous for life and we spent much of our time laughing and wandering about her neighborhood. She did not have a car, and her mother worked full time as a single parent. Sonja was a student at the University in Sao Paulo and wanted to become an actress. Her life was modest by comparison in Brazil; however, Sonja later became a star in a Brazilian soap opera

On a warm day, Sonja introduced me to her friends as we attended a small carnival full of vendors, booths, games, rides and music. As we walked about, I found a vendor who engraved jewelry. I was wearing the bracelet that my wing-man, Luciano, had given me during our flight to Brazil. I decided to have my name engraved on the top, and the date I received the bracelet on the back. Sonja was intrigued.

The small-town event reminded me of childhood memories at my grade school. In fourth grade I attended a carnival in our auditorium and it was also filled with booths, games, music, and a cakewalk. It still made me chuckle when I thought of my mother's face when I brought two cakes home.

I can still hear the music as I walked around and around the chairs. I could not resist and dragged Sonja to participate in a cakewalk.

As I looked up at Sonja, my mouth dropped open. I had won a cake and would be taking it home for her family. I gathered up my finished, engraved bracelet. Sonja and I made the walk back to her home. I shared with Sonja how I came to meet Luciano, and my last encounter with him.

Luciano and I had the opportunity to dine for lunch on a beautiful Brazilian afternoon. Mamai was not too happy when he arrived at our home. He was someone new, and her lifted eyebrow, and characteristic frown, warned me to be cautious. We drove to a nice café in Sao Paulo, and we reminisced about our meeting in Los Angeles on the plane.

Luciano expressed a desire to marry an American girl. "Why?" I asked. His response, "Because they have divorce in America."

I thought this was a ridiculous reason to marry, however out of respect, I continued listening to this narcissistic Brazilian man. I noticed he often looked at his reflection at every opportunity. It dawned on me that he looked a great deal like Gene Wilder.

Luciano was planning to attend a wedding in Italy and invited me to be his date. The wedding was in September, and I could fly to Italy from Bogota and then return to the states after the wedding. Luciano offered to pay for my flight and accommodations while in Italy. I was taken back by this offer.

As Sonja and I continued our walk home, she expressed a concern and recommended I ask my Brazilian father to investigate this man's background. I agreed, and we both marveled at the thought of my traveling to Italy. *"How is your Italian?"* Sonja asked.

I PLACED THE SMALL BLANKET ON MY LAP AS I SETTLED INTO MY LONG-anticipated flight. The idea of a trip to Italy raised my eyebrow, and then I raised my right upper lip (just like my sister Katie) and giggled.

.

CHAPTER 31

*T*he flight was calm, and the sound of the captain announcing our arrival brought anticipation for a new day. I looked down at my bracelet from Mr. Luciano and smiled. We landed in Caracas, and I was escorted into a large room surrounded by windows. The ground crew was very kind and explained that I would be waiting here for my next flight. My Spanish was not very good, but Portuguese helped. We seemed to understand each other nicely.

I settled into my four-hour wait, retrieving a book I purchased in Sao Paulo. I opened *Doctor Zhivago* by Boris Pasternak. It was a long book, and I had always wanted to read it. As I began, from over the edge of the cover, I saw three young men looking at me. They seemed intrigued. I smiled at them, and they spoke to each other in a language I did not recognize. They were all tall and had Scandinavian features. I wondered where they were from? I was surprised when they approached me. They spoke to me using hand gestures, motioning toward my book. I had no idea what they were saying. I glanced at the cover of *Dr. Zhivago*; I smiled and spoke to them in Portuguese. They seemed very confused and walked away.

I focused on my book and continued with Boris Pasternak's story.

I sunk deep in my chair and forgot about the world revolving around me, and the tall Scandinavian young men. Hours passed when beams of sunlight radiated across the room. The sun rose (as did I), and as I looked up and closed my book, I witnessed a radiance of light. Outside the large picture windows, the brilliant blue sky was land-scaped with pink and white clouds. The light revealed mountains that protruded with canine peaks. I walked over to the windows, my eyes fixed, and I marveled in its majesty. Never had I experienced such beauty in a sunrise.

The announcement over the loudspeakers alerted me of my departure. I gathered up my bags, book, hat and began my walk to the gate. I was again escorted the entire time by more ground personnel. They must have seen me as very young and in need of help. I was without a wing-man and I appreciated the special attention.

I boarded a much smaller aircraft, and I was instructed to sit in the back area of the plane. All passengers were seated towards the front or the back; no one sat in the middle. I suspected a weight and balance issue, or perhaps a center-of-gravity adjustment? I pondered this as I gazed out of my window, taking in the breath-taking mountains.

We rolled out onto runway 09L and stopped. The engines wound up, and I realized we were about to execute a full-power take off. The engines continue winding to full power, and the pilot released the brakes. As we powered down the runway, the plane began to shake; bags shifted around the cabin. The pilot rotated back, and we climbed out in the steepest ascent I have ever experienced. The tray tables fell open from the backs of the seats, and I noticed two nuns praying as they crossed their chest in the name of the Father, the Son, and the Holy Spirit.

I smiled and thought, "Wow, what would father think of this!" We climbed out of this beautiful place, and I took in the surrounding mountain range Cerro El Avila, with an elevation of 7,200 feet. The airport sat 236 feet above sea level. It was an exhilarating climb, and as we leveled off, the engines reduced power, and people on the airplane quieted down.

Our flight time was about two hours, and it wasn't long before we approached El Dorado International Airport in Bogota, Colombia. Bogota sat at an elevation of 8,360 feet. I looked out my window and saw the airport runway 13L, and I buckled up for our landing. As we made our final approach, it was early morning, and I noticed the wet ground beneath, hinting that it had rained. The sound of our engine slowed to a stop. We arrived safely answering the prayers of the nuns. I felt anxious to see my Colombian sister Luna and meet her family.

The terminal was full of people holding signs. I looked around for Luna, but I was quickly escorted to a room for inspection. My luggage waited for me there, and the custom officers inspected the contents of my bags and asked numerous questions. After satisfying customs, I walked to an open area and saw Luna alongside her father. She smiled her big familiar smile. I ran into her embrace. I was so tired and happy to be there. Her father looked like a pleasant man. He was small and had white hair. His brown eyes had a sparkle that emanated kindness. We walked to his car and made the drive into town and to my new temporary home.

The clouds prevented the sun from drying the streets. The quantity of stop lights increased as we neared the busy streets of Bogota. The sound of the windshield wipers slapped back and forth, while the smell of rain was heavy in the air. When we stopped, a group of young boys walked in between the cars selling cigarettes. They tapped on our windows and held up packs of Marlboros. Luna told me that sometimes they sell flowers or candy. I could see the Andes Mountains in the distance as we traveled through the Historical District, La Candelaria. I saw boxes. There were pink ones, green ones, blue ones, and yellow ones, and they all looked the same. It was beautiful.

The Columbian rain continued to hit our windshield as we made our drive to Luna's home. They had a small grocery market beneath their flat where Luna's mother was busily working. We climbed the stairs and arrived where Luna's brother was waiting. Carlos was a small shy boy.

Luna and I shared a small room with two twin beds. There were windows that overlooked a courtyard housing boxes of fruits, vegetables, and inventory items for the market. The flat was comfortable, and the living room had a big picture window overlooking the main street, or Calle.

The family was warm toward me. I did not speak Spanish very well; however, the Portuguese was helpful, and within a few weeks, I was getting the hang of speaking Spanish.

Luna and I spent each day on some kind of adventure. I had only one month in Bogota, so Luna and I spent every day doing something. It was never boring, and I loved the unfamiliar places to visit and explore. My Colombia father, Juan, joined us, acting as our personal chauffeur. I think he enjoyed taking us here and there and getting away from the market.

When Luna's father didn't escort us, we took buses and walked around Bogota. Bogota had the highest crime rate comprised of small children. It was not uncommon to have a child run up to you and take your purse. They lived in the sewers stretched beneath the city for miles. The urchins appeared at daylight and disappeared at nightfall. Luna and I would always put our money in our socks and never carried a bag.

We traveled to the Gold Museum, in the heart of Bogota. It was filled with ancient Tumbaga gold from pre-Columbian civilizations; conquistadors. As we entered the building, we were escorted by security into a small room. The room was dark, and the entrance door closed. We stood in a dark room, and soft music began to play as the lights gradually warmed, giving the effect of the sun rising. Our eyes were met with the brilliance of gold. We turned 360 degrees in the center of a gold universe. It was magnificent! Almost as beautiful as the Venezuelan sunrise.

We toured the Salt Cathedral of Zipaquirá. It was an underground Catholic cathedral. My Columbian father (or Popi as he became known) and Luna walked with me as we descended into the cathedral. The air thinned, and I could smell the cold salty dampness secreting from the walls. People from Colombia made this visit each Sunday for mass. I thought how much I enjoyed the Roman Catholic church for its antiquities and traditions. There was a familiarity standing in the quiet, solus environment. I observed Popi as he made the sign of the cross over his chest. I stood quietly and scanned the walls, ceiling and floor. I closed my eyes.

Time seemed to stand still and my memory of this moment nestled far away. We traveled beyond this salt mine and on to our next tourist attraction.

"Come on Tess," Luna shouted at me as we stood in line to board a tram. The tall majestic mountain of Monserrate had a sanctuary overlooking Bogota. The tram was old and held only a few people with each trip. Popi, Luna and I traveled up the mountain to spend a day taking in the sights.

There was a flea market in full view as we exited the tram. Many merchants sold their goods and a small group of men played acoustic music. Being an inquisitive person, I would stop and look at everything for sale. I spoke Portuguese/Spanish and mixed up the words. People appeared confused when conversing with me. Luna laughed, "Tess, you look American, but you speak Spanish with a Brazilian accent!" I beamed and dropped my shopping bag. As I bent over to pick it up, I noticed a familiar pair of boots; brown suede waffle stompers. They were American. I looked up to see a handsome man staring down at me.

I smiled when he asked, "Do you speak English?"

"Yes," I replied. I gazed into the green eyes of the stranger. He was so relieved to meet an American. He was traveling alone and only in Bogota for a couple of days.

"Where are you from?" he asked.

"I am from California," I said.

"So am I," he replied.

"I am from Northern California," I said.

"So am I," he replied.

We laughed, and I said, "I am from the San Francisco Bay Area."

"So am I," he replied, his eyes and mouth turning upward. As it turned out, we both grew up in San Leandro, and we both attended the same schools. We lived within blocks of each other, yet we had never met.

"How is that possible?" I asked him. His name was Samuel Gomez, and he was five years older than me. He was currently a law student at UC Davis in California.

Samuel had just left the United Nations convention in Caracas, Venezuela and made a stop in Bogota. We invited Samuel to join us for dinner in Luna's home that evening. He accepted, and we spent the entire day and evening together.

Samuel had the most fascinating eyes. They reminded me of cat eyes; no, not Cat Stevens! They were green, and the pupil was shaped like a football. It was a coloboma deformity of his iris from birth. It made it almost impossible not to stare into his eyes.

Samuel was a tall man with dark brown hair. I had grown accustomed to Latin attire and Samuel was a reminder of what awaited me back in the states. He was rugged looking with a typical American stature. Samuel carried his backpack and wore a baseball cap. Most American men did not have the style of Latin men, except for Elio. The cultures were very different. However, there was a familiarity in Samuel. He was from the Manor and we did grow up in the same small town nestled in the San Francisco Bay area. I welcomed our conversations in English.

We invited Samuel to spend the next day traveling to Villa de Leyva and the small village, Paipa. It was hot that day, as we maneuvered the small streets lined with stucco walls and dirt paths. Ladies opened hibachis', sizzled with corn on the cob, while slices of meat roasted on wooden sticks. Samuel and I stopped to sample the vendors recipes. By the time the sun set, Samuel felt like family to us. It was as though I had known him all my life.

Samuel departed from Bogota the next morning. Popi drove us to the airport. "See you in the States," I shouted as he boarded his flight. I watched as Samuel's airplane made the sweeping pass over the mountains of Monserrate, and into the clouds. Just like that, he was gone.

CHAPTER 32

$\mathcal{M}$y Columbian Mother, Isabella, was a kind, jolly woman that worked very hard in her grocery store. I would, on occasion, cashier for her; waiting on customers and bagging groceries. I sat on the stool in front of the register, thinking how different my life was in Colombia. I was in the middle here, much like home. I was comfortable working and helping as much as possible. There was a familiar pain in the eyes of Momi. It reminded me of my mother at home.

My Columbian family was kind to me. It was not a family of riches; it was a family filled with love. The family extended everything they had to me. We had a hot water heater that sat atop the kitchen counter. It held approximately five gallons of water. I learned how to take a very short shower and use only what was necessary. I complained about my weight because I gained a few pounds since arriving in South America. I said, "I have tres-barrigas," and Momi would laugh. She thought this was very funny, and it became my trademark. I was the American girl with tres-barrigas (three stomachs).

Not long after my arrival, Luna's older sister, Lina, came home to visit. Lina had married an American, and was residing in Seattle,

Washington. Lina resembled her mother, and she had the gleam in her eyes inherited from Popi. Lina was a warm addition, and her English was perfect. She taught Spanish in Seattle. We squeezed another twin bed in our room, and every night was a pajama party of three.

Lina and I spent countless hours talking about her adventures in the United States. She loved her husband very much. When she spoke of him, her eyes lit up. She said to me, "Tom, this, and Tom, that," and I listened into the wee hours of the night as we had lain on our beds and talked.

I shared my disappointments, and my anticipation of going back to America. I confessed my affections for Elio. I told Lina that he was too old for me. But I continued to imagine a life with him regardless of our age difference. It really did not matter to me.

Lina did not travel anywhere in Bogota without her umbrella. She used it to smack the child robbers on the head, if they attempted to grab her purse. It was amusing to walk by her side. She showed strength and carried herself with confidence. The three of us bounced around town together. We certainly enjoyed our food. We became a bit like my stomach, tres-barrigas.

Shopping was comprised of hand gestures and bartering. Many transit busses would travel by, as we stood on street corners. Diesel exhaust fumes spewed out of their tailpipes, causing me to cough.

My time grew short in Bogota and, as the sun would set, I would lie in my bed listening to the small transistor radio that rested upon the nightstand. I slowly turned the dial till I'd find an American song. I listened to the songs and one in particular grabbed my attention. A woman sang about a young boy in a nightclub. A stranger to her eyes. He was performing with just his guitar and his words reminded her of herself. As he sang, she became embarrassed and felt as though everyone in the club knew he was singing about her. "Killing Me Softly" I whispered as I fell asleep.

The next morning, I discovered a stairway in the courtyard that led to the rooftop. Our flat was a brick building, and the rooftop over-looked the city of Bogota.

"Come on Luna, let's go up", I exclaimed. Luna trailed behind as I climbed the stairs to her rooftop. It was a beautiful morning, and I wanted to explore. I looked about and asked why no one spent time up here? "It would be a wonderful terrace with trees, flowers and outdoor furniture," I suggested. There was only silence, and Luna began to cry. I sat down with her and listened as she unfolded the story of her baby brother, Adam. Her baby brother died on the terrace. He was just a toddler, and only two years of age.

He and his mother, Momi, were up here washing the family clothes. Momi used to wash clothes by hand in the brick basin we were leaning on and hang them to dry. When she turned to hang clothes on the clothesline, her brother fell into the washbasin; head first. She was not able to save him. The pain is too great for family members to visit the terrace.

The pain I observed in Momi's eyes suddenly became transparent. It was the loss of her son. It was the same pain in my Mother's eyes. Two women, who had never met, living worlds apart, shared the same loss. My brother's cause of death was different than his.

Donald had swallowed a small object he found on the carpet. It became lodged in his throat. His choking drew my mother's attention. Father was home, and fortunately he was able to apply pressure to his abdomen and dislodge the marble. Bleeding followed, and they rushed him to a nearby hospital. After numerous tests, Donald was admitted, and it was discovered he had an esophageal stricture. My parents elected to have surgery to correct the stricture. It was while Donald was in recovery; he developed a blood clot. The clot traveled from his arm into his superior vena cava. He immediately had a seizure and died.

I felt wedged between my two mothers and their pain. Luna, like me, also lost her younger brother. The pain stung as I stood next to my sister and I sensed familiarity; I was close enough to start running.

The radio blasted, waking me from my afternoon nap. Light streamed down on us and I heard the announcer's overly excited voice holler "SCORE," a football game unfolded on a nearby radio.

I leaned over and tapped Luna while she faded in and out of consciousness, "Wake up Luna," I said with a whisper.

CHAPTER 33

"*I* think tonight will be very special," I said to Luna. We were attending a basketball game. It was my last night in Bogota, and the USA men's NAIA (National Association of Intercollegiate Athletics) team is playing the Soviet Union. It was a sold-out game at the stadium. Luna, Lina, and I planned to walk from our home to the event.

It was a warm summer evening as we walked to the game. We passed an old brick Catholic high school that Luna and Lina had once attended. Luna, Lina and I arrived at the stadium and found our way to our assigned seats. I wore red, white, and blue to show my support, and Luna brought an American flag. We took our seats and waited for the game to begin.

The announcements were made, and the American team was introduced. The crowd was quiet as each player entered the court. I stood to show my support, and I observed the surrounding crowds remained seated.

When the Soviet Union players entered, the crowds cheered and stood. I stood as well to show my respect. As my eyes scanned the players, they were introduced one by one. I couldn't help sensing how familiar they looked to me.

It didn't take long before I recalled the airport in Caracas, Venezuela. The players were the same young men who were intrigued and attempted to converse with me about my book, *Dr. Zhivago*. They were the Soviet Union NAIA basketball team. "No wonder they were so tall," I thought to myself. I was elated to see them on the floor playing my home team.

A whistle blew, and I watched USA's shooting guard make a basket. I watched the game, while the memories grew thick and the entire stadium transformed into a gymnasium of students.

IT WAS A WARM SUMMER EVENING WHEN ANDRE AND I WATCHED MY high school basketball team play Andre's high school team. My high school team was superior to his, and I smiled when they maneuvered back and forth across the court. Andre snuck a kiss in between calls, whistles, and horns blowing. Basketball was so exhilarating to watch.

MY MIND FADED IN AND OUT OF MEMORIES, AND UNEXPECTEDLY I HEARD the final horn sound. Team USA was not doing well against the Russians. I sat down next to Luna and reminisced on the color of Andre's eyes. I recalled his smile and the firmness of his grip as he held my hand. His skin was so soft and his smell. Luna smiled back at me. "I am here," I told myself, "Enjoy the moment."

We, the USA, lost the game that night. The team left the stadium defeated, and I was surprised how the Columbian people behaved toward the American team. Luna and I felt as though we were the only people cheering for the USA team. We yelled and clapped when they scored a point, and people glared at us. When the Soviet Union scored a point, the stadium went crazy!

I asked Luna why the popular support was not for America? She proceeded to explain that Columbians felt Americans were a spoiled society. They had everything they wanted. They negatively regarded

Americans. The revelation made me sad. She continued to explain how the Soviet Union had a society of equality. They were equal in all they earned, acquired, and desired. This was more pleasing to the Columbian people; "Although," Luna explained, "Columbians will go to America, given the opportunity." It was confusing to me, and I did not understand their mindset.

As we made our way home, my mind wandered to the airport in Caracas. *Dr. Zhivago* was not allowed in the Soviet Union. Perhaps the team was commenting on this fact. Perhaps they recognized my American stature. I looked back with regret for the lost moment or opportunity. We sat so close in that airport. We occupied the same stadium and returned to our hotels and flats within the same city. We later returned to our respective countries, thousands of miles away from each other.

And just like so many others during my travels, we would never see each other again.

CHAPTER 34

"Go ahead and select the lobster you want!" Elio insisted. Scomas Restaurant was the oldest fish grotto in the city. They had a large tank of lobsters to select from. I smiled and tapped lightly on the tank, pointing to a nice-sized fellow.

Elio and I sat right in front of a large window looking out onto the bay. It was a romantic night. I hung onto every word that passed from his mouth. He leaned over and offered a taste of our appetizer. "When will I see you again?" he asked. The memory of Andre caused confusion to set in again.

After dinner, we drove through the streets of San Francisco in Elio's black Porsche, and I gazed at the houses. Little boxes one by one, I saw the colors. I thought of Father and of me sitting on his lap while he sang. I smiled. I glanced over my right shoulder, into the outside rear-view mirror, and saw the twinkling of the city lights in the distance. I looked at Elio and leaned toward him, turning up the volume on the radio.

THE SONGS ON THE RADIO WOKE ME FROM MY SLEEP, AND I REALIZED I was dreaming. The sun had not risen yet, and I gazed at the moon waxing on the windows' edge. "I will see Elio in a few days," I thought, and his image brought happiness to my heart.

My waning memory of Andre flitted to mind. I left Brazil without the love of Andre. I was there for him, and a hint of disappointment set in. *How could I have been so wrong?* As I reflected, I thought about being sixteen when I first met Andre, and fourteen when I first met Elio. *Would that make Elio my first love? Or would Andre be my first?* The memory of a first never seems to leave your heart. It was at that moment that I saved a small corner in my heart for that love, and only that love.

THE HISS OF BRAKES AND THE SOUNDS OF THE CITY GREW SOFTER AND softer. Our station wagon was filled with luggage and passengers. The boys in the streets, selling cigarettes, became smaller in the rear-view mirror. Lina and I would travel together for my return to San Francisco, California. I welcomed the company and looked forward to having Lina stay in my home.

"Home," I whispered to myself. I remembered my girlfriends from high school. I could still see Luna walking down the hallway, near our high school library. We always greeted each other and had lunch together in the cafeteria. Luna and Sofia were a big part of my high school years. Was I now a part of their life in South America?

"LET'S ALL GO TO PLANNED PARENTHOOD AND GET ON THE PILL," Darcie announced one day in the high school bathroom. We all congregated there for a smoke between classes. I pondered as I exhaled and extinguished my cigarette. It was not long until a group of us were crowded into Darcie's Corvair driving to Planned Parenthood in Hayward, California. I watched a traffic signal turn red through her dirty windshield. A bus passed by, and the diesel exhaust left a puff of dark smoke.

~

SMOKE COAXED ME FROM MY MEMORY AS I WATCHED A BUS PASS BY. Leaving Bogota was bitter sweet. My eyes focused on the airplanes flying into the airport ahead. I tracked their course as they faded in and out of clouds.

When we arrived at the El Dorado International Airport, the moment of sadness set in as I said goodbye to Popi and Momi and my Colombian family. I hugged and kissed them, taking extra time to embrace Luna. She was my dearest Columbian sister, and I missed her already.

I stared at Luna, memorizing her big brown eyes and long brown hair. A tear fell from her eyes.

"Besos," she said. I quietly turned and walked down the airport ramp. This time, I did not look back.

CHAPTER 35

$\mathcal{L}$ ina and I found our assigned seats and settled in for a long journey home. We were scheduled to stop in Panama City, Mexico City, and then Los Angeles. I looked out of my window and admired the sun rise over the mountain range in Bogota. It reminded me of a sunset over the mountain range in Rio de Janeiro. Bogota had a statue of the Virgin of Guadalupe high on the mountain top, and Rio had the statue of Jesus Christ the Redeemer. Both cities had a tram that streamed across the mountains taking tourists to wonderful historical sites.

As I gazed at the Virgin of Guadalupe from my aircraft window, I thought of Rio and my Brazilian family.

"TESS, LOOK HERE!" MY ATTENTION WAS INTERRUPTED BY MY BRAZILIAN sister, Elena. We climbed the stairs on the beautiful Corcovado mountain and stood before Jesus Christ the Redeemer. It was a beautiful evening in Rio de Janeiro. My family and I had traveled by car to Rio for a few days. The clouds surrounded the statue of Christ with a slight stratus layer formation. I laughed at Elena as she posed for a photograph in front of the statue. As the sun set, Christ became illuminated by floodlights that surrounded the base of the figure. It was breathtaking. I was overcome with the powerful presence. Sofia rolled her eyes and glanced away from Elena.

∽

"Fasten your seatbelts and return your seats to the upright position as we prepare for departure." I looked about the cabin and felt our aircraft push back. I watched as the ground crew motioned the flight crew that all was clear and we began our taxi to the departure runway. My trip was filled with many wonders of the world. I smiled at Lina as we rolled out, moving faster and faster down the runway. Within a few seconds, we climbed up into the morning sky, and I allowed the tears to flow. I looked down at the airport below us and waved goodbye, though I was sure that no one on the ground could see me.

I slept on our way across Colombia to Panama City. I woke only for the shortstop to pick up passengers. We continued our trip across Central America and into the twilight hour. The rumbling sound of the engines put most passengers to sleep. I stared out of my window, into the ambiguity of time, and admired the twinkle of the stars and searched for the moon. "We should be crossing the equator soon," I thought as I looked down in wonder. Cuba was down there, somewhere, surrounded by the Caribbean Sea.

"I am up here," I shouted within myself to all the souls below. I am above another civilization at 30 thousand feet looking down, and I thought of myself sitting on the bench at the Marina. I would look up and fantasize who was aboard those jets landing in Oakland.

I leaned over and gazed towards the cabin and wondered who was flying our airplane? Would I ever sit in the captain's seat of an airline cockpit and fly? What did my future hold? One thing was sure, my future no longer had Andre in it. I let out a deep breath and stared at the stars. I did not close my eyes. I then grabbed a Life magazine, that was left in the seat pocket ahead of me, and skimmed through it. I stopped to admire the *Campbell's Soup* advertisement.

Dinner was served at dusk on the airplane. Passengers began to move about, and I continued staring at the soup can, deep in thought. I finally stirred when I became aware of the flight attendant handing me a hot towel. As I wiped my face, I welcomed the smell of coffee, and the steak dinner placed on the tray before me. Lina and I enjoyed our food and talked about the stop in Mexico City. After dinner, I cast my eyes out the window again and watched lightning strikes in the distant sky, wondering how the weather might impact our landing.

Mexico City International Airport sat 7,316 feet above sea level. I wished I had a compass to help navigate my future; as we approached our final path on runway 05L into Mexico City. The weather was very cloudy, so I prepared for a bumpy landing. Lina looked to me for comfort and direction, and I reassured her with my smile. "Let's watch the wheels," I said. As the wheels near the ground, I whispered, "Closer, closer, closer," and then, bam, we touched down. I leaned over to Lina and exclaimed, "Good landing," as she returned my smile.

Lina and I were instructed to wait in a room outside the departure gate, along with many passengers waiting to board our airplane to Los Angeles. As we waited, we watched the lightning in the sky. It was quite the light show, and I knew it was a matter of safety that we needed to hunker down and wait it out. I recalled my ground school instructor explaining weather, and the effect it could have on aircraft performance. He emphasized lightening typically will not cause damage to airplanes; however, lightening from severe weather storms can make for a very turbulent flight.

I found myself missing Brazil and Colombia. My heart ached as I moved further and further away from the countries I came to love. The mixture of life in South America and the uncharted life that had yet to be discovered, assured me of: nothing. I no longer would be cared for by my father and mother and live in the ticky-tacky home I grew up in. I would be expected to make my own way.

As I stood staring out the windows of Mexico City International Airport, I heard music by Led Zeppelin and I sang to myself, "Going to California." And then I remembered my father singing, "Boxes, little boxes." Memories of sitting in the right seat of Father's airplane as we took off from Hayward Airport. I was overlooking California's bay area with rows and rows of boxes; and they all looked the same.

LUCIANO CREPT INTO MY MIND, AND I REMEMBERED HOW PAPAI WENT to so much trouble to investigate my Brazilian wing-man. The prospect of traveling to Italy with him was a hot topic of discussion.

Papai came home one evening, and we sat at the dining room table for our formal dinner. Papai said, "Luciano comes from a very wealthy family Tess. He has lots and lots of money. There is no problem if you go to Italy with this man." I looked around the table for some kind of reaction on my family's faces. They all began, one by one chattering in Portuguese, waving their hands about, and in a volume, that I construed as angry. Sofia seemed to be the most concerned. She was the guard at my front gate, and always had my best interest at heart. In a dramatic show, Papai stood, slammed his hands on the table, and silenced everyone. Time stood still, and then my sweet sister Nê, looked at me and said, "Well, Tess, all you have to lose is your virginity," and then she smiled.

"FLIGHT #268 HAS BEEN DELAYED," THE ANNOUNCER PROCLAIMED OVER the intercom. A general sound of disapproval moved through the room of passengers. We were packed in like a herd of cattle. It was hot, and people were babbling in Spanish. The weather was the cause of our discomfort, and I turned to Lina, "It's mesmerizing," I whispered. She smiled and we both returned to watching the lightning strikes.

"Papai what shall I do?" I looked into my Brazilian father's brown eyes for an answer as he clenched his pipe between his teeth. Our after-dinner caffeine and nicotine fix were the perfect time to get Papai to myself. He sat pensively, and with a deep sigh replied, "You are going to have to make this decision yourself." He reached into his coat pocket and handed me a gift.

"What's this?" I asked.

Papai smiled, "Open it."

I unwrapped a hand carved tobacco pipe. It was uniquely shaped in a half moon and the mouth tip rotated around to make a full moon.

"You can put it in your pocket," Papai said with a wink. I was elated with my new pipe. "It's Italian," he added.

Luciano was Italian.

"It is settled, I am not going to Italy," I asserted. I packed my pipe with fine Brazilian tobacco, and struck a match to light my new pipe.

A large lightning bolt transformed the silhouette of Mexico City, into a bright purple sky. I knew I made the right decision. Luciano was not upset when I gave him my answer. He did not seem surprised or alarmed. Luciano faded away much like the airplanes that took off at the Oakland Airport. They take off, climb into the sky and disappear. And so, did he.

CHAPTER 36

"All passengers, please board flight #268 to Los Angeles."

Lina and I were all too happy to comply. With cattle-like formation, the passengers all moved forward one by one into a Pan American 747 for our final flight home.

It is interesting how we unwaveringly take instructions from speakers. We moved in single file, patiently awaiting our turn to take our seats. Passengers can be very miserly. I observed passengers claiming temporary ownership of the overhead bins. There were passengers who invaded *space*. There were passengers who put their feet on the bulkhead and left their footprints and filth behind. There were passengers who disrespected our flight attendants.

I grew more anxious as Lina and I got closer to home. I nervously leafed through my magazine. I became fidgety and stopped at the familiar advertisement and lingered. We were behind schedule coming in to Los Angeles and I feared we would miss our connection to San Francisco. My original arrival date was changed, and I planned on calling my parents when we arrived in Los Angeles.

My eyelids grew heavy as I shifted my thoughts from the ignoble passengers, to the humble children of Brazil. Roberta Flack's singing filled my headphones, and I slowly drifted off as my mind dipped up and down like the wooden roadrunner in my Uncle's café.

∼

"I HAVE A SURPRISE TESS" ELIO SAID AS WE DROVE TO HIS HOME IN HIS black Porsche. It was a cold rainy evening in March, and we had just returned from a party. Elio had a small home in the Hayward hills, and the party wasn't far from there. We parked in his garage, alongside his Harley Davidson, and entered a cold house. Elio dropped his leather jacket on the floor, pulled off his boots, tossing them across the room, and lifted me up in the air. I gazed up at the ceiling, as my stomach became smothered by his kisses. He embraced me and lowered my body, drawing my lips closer to his. Our eyes fixed, and he kissed me. His need matched mine. My breath increased in intensity as Elio began to unbutton my blouse. "I have some bubble bath," he whispered.

"Let's take a bath," I smiled, and dashed off to the bathroom. I drew the water as my love returned with a bottle of wine and two wine glasses. Elio lit candles and staged them perfectly around his bath tub. I removed his pressed shirt, moving my hands to his belt and his slacks. I ran my hands through the hair on his chest, and kissed him gently on his lips, allowing his breath to take me in. I moved to kiss his neck and his chest. Elio swept me up and lowered me into the tub of foamy water. No other thoughts interrupted my feelings and thoughts of him. I was suspended in his arms.

"I leave for Brazil tomorrow," I whispered to Elio. We sipped our wine and listened to the sweet sound of Marvin Gaye in the background.

"I will be here when you return," he reassured me.

I studied the *Campbell's Soup* art work by Andy Warhol, which hung adjacent to us. Elio's bathroom walls were painted a light blue, with white puffy clouds floating between the displayed pop art. "How odd. Who would have thought a can of tomato soup could become so famous?" I mentioned as I sank deeper into the warm water, and against his chest.

I picked up a sea sponge, and gently washed Elio's hands, and then his arms. I turned to wash his chest, when he took the sponge into his hand, and gently washed my back. His hand and sponge become one as they followed the curves of my shoulders, leading down to my breasts, and stopped at my belly. I felt exposed for the first time in my life.

Elio helped me out of the tub and wrapped me in a big towel. He carried me to his bedroom, and I could hear the record change to the soft tone of Barry White. Elio kicked his cowboy boots out of the way, causing us to chuckle. He gently lowered me on to his bed, and for the first time we manifested our passionate love to each other.

～

"PLEASE FASTEN YOUR SEAT BELTS," STARTLED ME AS I STARED AT THE magazine. We were landing soon, and I had a warm thought accompanying me as I returned to America. Los Angeles was only 20 minutes away.

CHAPTER 37

"What do you mean you are late?" Sofia asked as we sat in our bedroom.

I had been in Brazil for three months and my menstrual cycle decided to take a diversion. "I am late," I said, "What should I do?" Sofia and I decided to speak with my Brazilian mother.

Mamai looked down at me and frowned and then looked up at me. I briefly saw my Grandpa's face peering down at me. "Let's go for a drive," she said.

Mamai drove Sofia and me to a local pharmacy. Mamai spoke to the pharmacist at length, and I had no idea what they said to each other. I was soon taken to a back room, and the pharmacist arrived with a syringe and a vial. The pharmacist closed the drape, making the room feel like a dressing room at a local boutique. Sofia sat next to me, explaining that I will get an injection and my cycle will begin in three days. If it does not, then I am pregnant.

Mamai stood between the drape and me, rambling on and on in Portuguese. She spoke loud enough for me to hear and repeated over and over that I will be shipped back to America if I am pregnant. She began naming men that had stopped by our home, one by one, as though I had sexual contact with each and every one of them.

Voices and accusations without truth rang from my past. I was deeply insulted by her assumptions, and I attempted to explain how wrong she was. I sat in silence, imagining her arms flailing about. Her Portuguese words numbed my ears. I felt like a child again. I felt shame.

It was three long days with no results. Mamai, Sofia, and I returned to the local pharmacist for a second injection. "This time you should have results," Mamai said with one eyebrow raised. I stared at her eyebrow, noting that she was able to raise one or the other at any given time. I said nothing during the long drive home. It was pointless.

I waited another three long days, and then my cycle arrived. My Brazilian mother, Sofia, and I were all relieved. The welcome of cramping, pain, and heavy flow confined me to my room all day, that evening, and into the night. I missed our formal dinner and my after-dinner smoke with Papai. I had no idea what they gave me or what happened to me, but it worked. I spared my honorable Mamai any embarrassment or humiliation from her American daughter, the wild child.

I thought of Papai. "Will you fix me an American breakfast?" my Brazilian father asked me. He imagined my breakfast in the states and I laughed and said, "Ok, one day I will make you an American breakfast!" I never cooked that breakfast for him, although I wish I had.

I laid in bed thinking about the evening as it unfolded without my company. I had wanted a future with Andre; however, I missed the comfort and security with Elio. A tear ran down my face. "Where am I and what am I doing here?" I asked myself.

～

I GAZED OUT OF THE BEDROOM WINDOW AS IT TRANSFORMS INTO AN airline window. It is dark outside, and the lights of the city began to appear. The twinkling Los Angeles illuminated below me as the aircraft engines reduced power. I looked out and watched as the flaps deployed, signaling our descent into LAX.

I imagined the captain and the first officer sitting in the cockpit exchanging commands to each other, while listening to the air traffic controller. The lights on runway 6L became brighter as we made our left base to final approach. I glanced over at Lina with a thumbs-up gesture and smiled. I focused on the wheels as we move closer and closer to the runway. My heart beat faster, and my pupils became larger. When the tires touched down, the plane rocked back and forth, and the pressure of heavy braking threw us back into our seats. We continued skidding down the wet surface. It seemed to take forever until we finally settled to a slow stop.

As we waited to proceed with taxi instructions from ground control, I looked out my window and then back at Lina and I said, "That was not a perfect landing."

CHAPTER 38

*M*amai looked down at me with her stern expression, "Tess we are the first to fly, not the Wright Brothers, it was Alberto Santos-Dumont in 1906!" As I looked up at Mamai, I nodded my head and agreed (it was always best to agree). As we walked about this magnificent aeronautical museum in Sao Paulo, I was enchanted with the vintage aircraft. I stood in awe of the 14-Bis biplane photo that Alberto Santos-Dumont flew for a distance of 197 feet. I read a sign next to it stating, "Brazil is first to fly, not the United States."

"Oh my," I said to myself. "They take this stuff seriously." I wondered why my history classes did not discuss the event and its controversy. In any case, I enjoyed all the historical airplanes. My time was nearing to an end, and I loved that my family wanted to share the museum of flight with me during our journey from Rio de Janeiro to Sao Paulo. As I read through the displayed narration of the first flight, Mr. Santos-Dumont did not have a perfect landing either.

I POKED MY HEAD INTO THE COCKPIT AS I EXITED THE PLANE, "THANK you Captain for a good flight," I said with a smile. Captain Pan American gave me a thumbs-up and smiled back.

Lina and I walked through Los Angeles terminal, and I was abruptly escorted into a large room sheltering long tables. A man motioned me over to one that was empty, with a woman standing guard. My luggage had been placed neatly on the floor, and he signaled me by snapping his fingers to put my bags on the table. I immediately complied, and the woman unpacked my property for inspection. I looked up for Lina, and she was gone. I was alone with the custom control agent, and I did not understand why.

As the agent unpacked nine months of stuff, she asked where I purchased each item. One by one, I answered each question, and then she found my pipe. "What have you smoked in this?" she asked.

"Tobacco," I answered.

"We shall see," she responded as she motioned a man over. "Send this down for inspection," she told him. It took me a minute to realize that I had been profiled as a drug smuggler. The pipe was only the first item to warrant intense scrutiny. The agent inspected my platform shoes, wallet, and the lining of my coat. "Where did you purchase this coat?" she asked. The inside lining had a label disclosure, "Made in Istanbul, Turkey."

"I bought this jacket in California," I explained.

"Where in California?" she asked with one eyebrow raised.

"In Hayward, California," I respectfully replied.

"Where in Hayward, California?" she asked.

"At a store named Noby in a mall called Southland Mall," I said.

"Good thing I know this mall," her evil eyes narrowed. They widened again when she came across a bottle of lavender liquor I had purchased in Bahia. "What is this?" she asked.

"It's a bottle of liquor that I purchased in Brazil, it's a gift," I said.

"You are not old enough to have liquor," she responded.

"I purchased it in Brazil, and the legal age is 18 in Brazil," I said.

"You are in California now, and the legal age is 21!" she responded. She confiscated the bottle.

Passengers from many International flights passed through the room, while my search was conducted. The interrogation continued for endless hours, and my mind reminded me of my connection into San Francisco. "I am going to miss my flight," I said as a phone rang next to the custom agent. The agent answered the phone, and it was obvious that someone was questioning her as to why she was detaining me? She made the remark that she thought she had something here and hung up the phone. A man reappeared with my pipe and whispered in Miss Custom Control's ear.

"You can go," she reluctantly said, "But not until you pay $45.00 in duty tax."

I estimated she added up the purchases I had made abroad, and I paid her with my traveler's checks, while tears streamed down my face. Rattled, I half expected a physical exam. Cocaine was a huge problem and having just returned from Bogota, I made a perfect target. "Pack your bags," she said, grabbing my bottle of liquor. She handed my pipe to me and walked away in a huff.

Time stood still as hours ticked by. I glanced down at the long table with my belongings strung about for all the world to see. "Can I help you?" I looked up to see a captain in uniform. "Have you missed your flight?" he asked.

"Yes, I am traveling to San Francisco," I said.

Captain Angel helped me pack my luggage, and we tossed it on a conveyor belt. My luggage made the journey downstairs to a baggage carousel, while Captain Angel took out a black book from his flight bag.

His eyes scanned through pages and pages and then stopped. "If you hurry, there is a flight on Western Airlines at midnight to San Francisco," he said.

I stared at the four stripes on Captain Angel's jacket as we rode the escalator downstairs. My eyes settled on his cleft chin, and the fullness of his lower lip. His upper lip was framed with a pencil mustache, resembling Howard Hughes. His eyes were hazel, and his hair had traces of grey running through each strand that swept across his forehead. My guardian, Captain Angel, escorted me to baggage claim.

I spotted the discombobulated Lina sitting on her luggage. "Where have you been?" she asked.

"In customs," I murmured as I shook from exhaustion and shattered nerves.

Captain Angel instructed us to take a cab over to domestic flights, which was about six-city blocks away. "Hurry," he instructed.

I gave Captain Angel a big hug and thanked him. His smell was so familiar. He paid for our airport shuttle. His four stripes glowed and the gleam in his eyes were perfectly etched into my memory. I watched out of the window as he faded into the distance and disappeared like so many others. It was different that time. Somehow, I knew he would resurface one day. I had no idea when. My eyes met Lina's, and I asked her, "What just happened?"

CHAPTER 39

"*L*et's go shopping," Andre's mother, Reeta, said as I wiped the sleep from my eyes. It was a beautiful day in Brazil, and the sun was shining. Andre was away at school that morning, studying at the University of Sao Paulo. It seemed everyone attended the same university.

It was four months since my arrival in Sao Paulo. I received an invitation from Andre asking me to spend time at his home. Reeta was itching to see me, and I needed a break in scenery. Her French/Brazilian quality lured me in. She did not have a daughter, so I became her daughter for one week. Although our time together was not what I had hoped for when I originally traveled to Brazil, I accepted what time I could have, and was thankful.

Reeta was a very sophisticated woman, and we dashed about from shop to shop on Rua Augusta. She purchased clothes, shoes, espresso coffee cups, and anything I stopped to admire. No sooner than I would express a fondness for something, she bought it. Although everything in Brazil had a captivating quality, on this day it was banking that I found most intriguing.

We boarded her red Ford LTD and were chauffeured to her bank. The bank had closed, but that did not stop Reeta. She walked up to the front door and waved at the guard inside. He immediately opened the bank for her, and only her. I waited in the car, but could not help noticing how she conversed with a gentleman inside. I reflected back to my bank in the United States. If the bank was closed, it was closed. Reeta's husband must have been more important than I ever imagined. She was treated like a diplomat.

Soon she reappeared, and we continued our excursion to the grocery store. "I want to make a favorite meal for you tonight," she said. It was fondue night, and that was my favorite meal with Andre. *How did she know?*

Andre arrived home that evening with his father. Reeta and I slaved in the kitchen over the stove, preparing vats of melted cheese. I was then tasked with the duty of slicing mounds of French bread for the cheese fondue, while Reeta made the salad. She lined the long dining room table with electric pots for each entrée. The servants oversaw the meat and fruit for each course. The noise in the kitchen was intoxicating as Reeta spouted off in French, and then Portuguese, and then English. I smiled at her, and wasn't always sure what she was saying, but her hand gestures filled in the blanks.

We gathered for our feast, and I attempted to bury my feelings for Andre. I inspected my baby blue bell bottoms, my blue jacket, and my white halter top and smiled. Reeta purchased the stylish outfit for me that day. We consumed wine with our cheese fondue. We drank more wine with our meat fondue. We sipped a nice port wine with our chocolate/fruit dessert fondue. We retired to the formal living room. This household did not smoke, and I missed my coffee and nicotine finale. The family babbled away in French, Portuguese, and occasionally in English.

I retired a bit intoxicated that night. I removed Andre's maroon sweater from my bag. I drew it in against my face and inhaled one last smell of the lingering cologne. I gently placed it on the nightstand. As I fell into my bed, the sound of paper crinkling beneath my pillow grabbed my attention. I tried to sober my mind as I read the note from Andre, but I became confused.

His room was next door. Andre softly tapped on the wall, and I froze. "Really?" I said to myself. The note claimed he still loved me. "Well this is interesting," I thought, remembering he still had a girl-friend. I looked up and heard more tapping on the wall. The shadow of my arm being pulled into another dark room lurked in my memory. I crinkled up the note and threw it against the wall, but the tapping continued louder and louder.

~

"COME ON TESS, HURRY," LINA EXCLAIMED WHILE TAPPING ON MY shoulder. We exited the shuttle and dragged our luggage to the Western Airlines counter, hoping we were not too late for the midnight flight. The ticket agent told us to hurry; the aircraft was scheduled to push back in 15 minutes. The gate was upstairs and so we ran. We ran up the escalator, and we ran down endless gangways. I was emotionally and physically exhausted when we finally arrived at the gate. The gate agent looked at our tickets and announced, "You just made it." We made our way through the doors and onto the ramp, just as they closed behind us. The flight attendant helped us locate our seats.

As Lina and I buckled in, the flight attendant leaned over and asked, "Where are you arriving from, you look frazzled!"

I responded, "We arrived from Bogota, Colombia and I was detained in customs."

"Oh my, did you manage to bring some cocaine?" she asked with her inquisitive eyes and big smile, awaiting my answer.

"Bite your tongue," I quipped.

"That's a drag," she said as I rolled my eyes.

I inspected my baby blue bell bottoms, blue jacket and white halter top. They were covered in sweat and wrinkled. "I am a mess, Lina," I said.

Lina smiled and whispered, "Almost home, Tess."

Just then I realized that I did not make that phone call to my parents. They had no idea we were on our way home.

I glanced towards the cockpit and noticed our captain and first officer as their door closed. My *cocaine* flight attendant took her jump seat. After reaching for the intercom she announced, "Welcome aboard Western Airlines, flight XY&Z, please bring your seats to their upright position and fasten your seat belts."

I chuckled to myself and reminisced; "Western Airlines. The only way to fly!"

CHAPTER 40

*A*ndre's American host family lived in Castro Valley, California. Their family was comprised of Mr. Magnoli, his wife Jackie, their one son, one daughter, and lots of foreign exchange students bouncing in and out of their lives. Mr. Magnoli formally held a job as a taxicab driver in San Francisco, and later becoming a schoolteacher, he married Jackie. Mr. Magnoli was jolly, his wife; intense. They were also directors for the "Youth for Understanding" program in the east bay.

It was Jackie who came to our home in San Leandro, just before Christmas 1971. She consulted with our family at the prospect of hosting an exchange student. I was on the fence at first, but after spending the evening looking at Brazilian snap shots of female students, we settled on a young girl named Sofia Braga. She seemed the perfect fit for our *average* family. Average is probably an understatement, however, when one grows up in chaos and constant upsets, it all becomes average.

Andre's American family fascinated me. I spent many evenings being entertained with music, food, laughter and dancing. They had a game room downstairs with a ping-pong table. It was the perfect place for fun. It was there that I was introduced to fondue.

I was invited over, and we sat on the floor in the living room. The room had a big picture window, with a view of the San Francisco Bay. Paul Mariot played on the stereo. There were pillows stationed about with a long tablecloth placed center of us. Mr. and Mrs. Magnoli were the champion entertainers. As I made myself comfortable on the floor, we devoured mounds of cheese, sizzling meat, followed by melted chocolate. We dipped pieces of banana, strawberry, angel food cake, etc. into the chocolate. It was heavenly. I found myself falling deeper and deeper in love with the Magnoli's Brazilian foreign exchange student.

In the early week of April, Andre's family invited me on a ski trip with their local church. It was spring skiing season, and record amounts of winter snow had fallen. I accepted the invitation, and the following weekend I found myself packing for a trip to Bear Valley Ski Resort. It was two nights and three days, and we were to stay in a cabin high in the Sierra Nevada mountains.

We traveled by car behind a caravan of vehicles from the church. Andre could not keep his mouth off mine. It seemed that every moment we were engaged in a lip lock session, and I was waiting for his parents to stop us or say something? No one did. Sometimes, I would be uncomfortable and pull away, but this only encouraged him.

We arrived at our destination. Six feet of snow and twilight greeted our weary travels. No one could drive their vehicles in; the roads were not plowed. So, a snowmobile ride was offered to get us to our cabin. Andre declined and said we would manage. Darkness settled in, and it didn't take long before we found ourselves knee deep in snow, and lost. We forged on and thank goodness there was a full moon; we had light and each other.

"Look Tess, there is only one moon. Whenever you look at the moon, you must remember me. We will always see the same moon." I had a warm feeling come over me. Andre continued to hold me close.

"I love you, Andre," I said.

"I loved you from the first time we met, Tess. I want to always love you. One day, you will be my wife." Andre said with a smile. His accent drew me in closer and closer. I wanted him more than anyone I had ever met in my life. I trusted Andre, and for the first time, I trusted a man.

"Please don't leave me, Andre. Tell me you will always be there, no matter what." I said, stopping to see his face. The moon shined on him, and he seemed to glow. His face was so young and tender, and his nose was red from the cold.

"I promise," he whispered gently, while kissing the tip of my cold nose.

We finally found a cabin, but it housed unfamiliar voices and faces. It felt like hours before we found ours. We finally could hear familiar voices as we approached the front door of another cabin. I was shivering from the cold, my feet were frozen, but I was relieved; that is until I looked up.

Mr. and Mrs. Magnoli stood at the front door. Jackie looked on us with an unforgiving frown. They were thankful to see us and then annoyed at us. We were not a very good example for the church group, and the look in their eyes was all I needed to feel ashamed. I feared they judged me unjustly, and there was nothing I could do to change the look on their faces. We had been gone for two hours, and of course, they thought the worst. All that kissing displayed in the car was not approved, and rather than speak aloud to Andre and me, their silence spoke volumes.

I settled into an evening by the fireplace in silence. I asked Jackie where we were going to sleep, and I was told that all the *kids* would sleep in the loft. I grabbed my sleeping bag and headed up to the loft, finding a place in the corner where I laid out my bag and pillow. As I got in line for the bathroom, Andre entered the loft. He proceeded to place his sleeping bag and pillow alongside mine. "I don't think that would be a good idea," I said to Andre.

He shrugged his shoulders and smiled. "Too bad," he said.

We all retired for the night. As I lay in my sleeping bag, Andre leaned over to kiss me good night. Andre knew nothing of soft kisses. He pounded me with his aggressive strength. His large hands held my head. I motioned for him to stop, but he continued. He moved over onto my sleeping bag, his breathing intensified, our bodies touching.

I froze. I laid lifeless, not knowing what to do. I loved him, but this felt so wrong. Suddenly an arm grabbed Andre, lifting him up. The pastor suddenly threw my sleeping bag open to examine me. I think he thought I was naked, and we were having sex. I was humiliated and angry with Andre. I ran to the bathroom and cried. I could hear a slight tapping on the door, and shadows of my past cast shame around me.

The nice pastor scolded Andre and brought my sleeping bag to me. "You can sleep downstairs," he said. Mr. Pastor and I made our descent down the stairs and into a bedroom with other girls my age. I wished I had known about this room first. I laid out my bag on the floor, shut the door, and fell asleep. I wanted to go home, but I was trapped in this cabin with scrutinizing eyes. In my mind, it felt awful.

I withdrew from Andre the next morning. I sat on the opposite side of the table while we ate breakfast. I would not speak to him, I felt humiliated and embarrassed. Jackie glared at me between bites of food, and it wasn't long before she motioned me to another room. Jackie ripped me up one side and down the other. The words ejected from her mouth bounced off the walls. I felt numb and sick to my stomach. Jackie said I was a disgrace to the church group, and she asked how could I have behaved that way?

"I did not do anything wrong," I whispered to her with my head down. It was useless, and I was forced to endure whatever came out of her mouth.

We skied that day. Andre followed me down the ski runs. We were both somewhat amateur skiers, but the day lightened and the sun melted the shame of the previous night. I found myself laughing and having fun again. Our walk back to the cabin was easier this time, and I insisted on walking with a group rather than just Andre. I moved about the cabin with other church members and stayed clear of him. I was finished with the looks and gestures of others.

As we made our drive home from Bear Valley ski resort, I was seated next to Andre in the back seat. I would not hold his hand or allow him to kiss me. Andre seemed frustrated as I sat in silence. It was a much quieter ride home. I listen to the radio and Jackie chatting with Mr. Magnoli.

I glared out of the car window as we traveled out of the Sierras' and into the central valley. I admired rows and rows of walnut orchards passing by. I paid close attention as I noticed they were planted in perfect formation.

~

MY PUPILS FOCUSED IN AND OUT, MUCH LIKE MY CAMERA LENS. Walnut Orchards turned into soft light blue taxi way markers. One by one they passed the wing tips' edge. Our pilot rolled out onto runway 06L. We soon lifted off into the dark sky.

"No more orchards," I whispered.

CHAPTER 41

*W*hen I was 13 years old, Grandpa George and Grandma Lea invited me to spend a summer with them in Idaho. I was reluctant; however, my parents encouraged me to go. There was a part of me that felt compelled to reconnect with them and perhaps have a pleasant experience.

I stayed on their farm in Gooding, Idaho. On a beautiful summer day, I awoke to the sounds of cowbells in the pasture that strung along the outside of my window. Grandma was preparing breakfast, and Grandpa sat in his easy chair smoking a pipe, reading the morning paper. I woke to the unforgettable smell of coffee brewing and bacon sizzling in the frying pan.

I arose, and we all took our seats at the kitchen table for a morning breakfast. "So, Tess, what are we going to do with you?" Grandfather spewed from his mouth.

I was taken back by his remark. *What was that about?*

He leaned over, looking at me with his spectacles teeter-tottering on the end of his nose. His eyes sized me up and down.

I shrugged and smiled. "I can work outside today," I said. I soon found myself riding the lawn mower, pulling weeds in the garden, watering the flowers, helping with laundry, ironing, and washing dishes. I worked from sunup until sundown each day. I looked forward to bath-time because it was my alone time.

The running warm water brought me back to my Aunt and Uncle and the big claw-foot bathtub. I smiled at the sweet memories of being in their home in Oakland. In Idaho, I collapsed into bed each night from shear exhaustion, listening to the cow bells move about in the darkness of the night.

It was not long before Grandma gave me a sewing project. I relished in making children's pajamas for Christmas gifts. Grandma had grandkids from another marriage, and I was the perfect seamstress.

Grandpa would occasionally take me over to my Aunt's home for a visit. She was my father's sister, and she and my uncle had many children; they were all boys. This made my grandfather nervous for some reason. He was uncomfortable with me being alone with my male cousins. I was confused why? My Grandfather had a very distorted view of women. I sensed he did not trust me or my judgement.

A few weeks after my arrival, Grandpa and Grandma decide to give me a break from the chores on the farm. We took a weekend drive to a rodeo. I felt good about the prospect of taking a road trip. All my male cousins were participating in a real hometown rodeo. They were true cowboys, and the anticipation of seeing them ride brought me a sense of joy.

Grandpa, Grandma, and I traveled to Mackay, Idaho for the big event. The trip was half a day's travel in the car and upon our arrival we checked into a local motel. It was not long afterward that we drove over to the stadium. In the grandstands I watched the announced riders one by one as they entered.

My uncle and his sons were among the announced riders, and I stood to cheer them on. Grandpa reminded me to sit down and behave. As the event went on, I felt ill. The heat and dust, along with the constant criticism, broke me down. I asked Grandma if she would take me back to the motel room, so I could rest. Grandpa piped in; "I will take her." He was agitated, as usual, but he took me to the motel.

Once we were alone in our room, my Grandpa interrogated me,

stopping only to light the pipe between his teeth. He asked me questions about boys at home. He closed the curtains and paced back and forth. He leaned over and switched on the lamp next to my bed. He asked how many boys I slept with. He asked if I was a virgin. "I will not take you to a doctor to find out if you are a virgin, because I don't want to waste my money," he shouted at me. I was from the city, and I must get straightened out. Grandpa felt that I was trouble, and surely a pretty girl cannot be a good girl. I buried my head in my pillow, crying.

I never responded to his accusations. I froze. I froze just like when my sister was taken in the darkness. I froze, just as I did that day, standing knee deep in snow. I could not believe that a loving grandfather would ever spew words like these from his mouth. He didn't love me. I hated him. I hated him along with the others.

I remembered my father peering down at me from the small window behind the locked door. "Why did you bring *her* here," his voice rang in my ears. I remembered Grandpa as he stood with the shotgun in his hand and cat parts projected throughout the yard. I remembered my mother crying hysterically after my brother died. And then Jackie. Jackie stood there looking down at me, shaming me. I want to go home. I want to go home.

I am not what he accuses me of. I am not what she accuses me of. I am not.

THE LUMBERING SOUNDS DURING OUR FLIGHT TO SAN FRANCISCO slowly increased. I continued staring into the distant sky, trying to shake memories from my mind. I was intent on new beginnings and thoughts of leaving the past behind pushed forward. I wondered what town we were flying over and I counted the small lights that twinkled from inside the homes of strangers.

CHAPTER 42

*I*t is not long before my *cocaine* flight attendant, made her way over to Lina and me. She offered me a Coca-Cola and threw bags of peanuts my way. She rambled on and on and asked questions about my travels. She was bubbly and quite beautiful. I considered the thought of becoming a flight attendant. I had no idea what I was going to do when I returned home. I looked out my airline window and gazed at the dark sky filled with stars from a familiar constellation.

Lina and I gabbed about our arrival at San Francisco Airport. We chattered about her life in Seattle. Lina, a devoted wife and teacher, had that familiar gleam in her eyes when she spoke. She reminded me of Popi, and a warmness settled in my heart. Lina and her husband, Tom, met in college while she studied in Seattle. She had not met my family yet, and I was looking forward to her staying a few days before returning to Seattle.

She was a comfort to have alongside me, much like I imagine an angel would be. We both laughed and talked about my "near miss" in customs. Lina had read, in the Bogota newspaper, that many Americans were arrested in customs for smuggling cocaine mere months before we arrived. They hid the drugs in their platform shoes, lining of garments, and even ingested a sealed plastic bag full of it. Physical searches were becoming more and more common. That was a near miss. It would have been humiliating for me and embarrassing for them if I had undergone a physical exam. I was squeaky clean, figuratively speaking. I felt like a stinking mess. My hair looked like a Luciano, and my clothes were drenched in perspiration.

Miss Cocaine announced our arrival at San Francisco International Airport. My eyes tracked our long final approach to runway 19R. Lights twinkled in the Bay Area and along the San Mateo Bridge. It was nearly 1:30 a.m. and the city had fallen into a slumber. Few vehicles passed over the bridge from Hayward to San Mateo. I peered in the direction of Hayward Hills and wondered, "How is my sweet Elio sleeping?"

The sound of the engines slowed, and I listened to the familiar sound of our flaps deploying. I buckled up, as time stood still over the breaks of water beneath us. We slowly descended, while gliding down to the black asphalt ahead of us. I waited in anticipation of our touch-down, and then the gentle squeak of rubber settled softly as we slowed to a stop. It was a perfect landing. My eyes teared up with joy.

Lina and I made our way down the empty aisle. Not too many were on the late-night flight. I stopped to complement our captain for a perfect landing. Captain Western Airlines, his first officer, and Miss Cocaine smiled and waved goodbye. I walked down the stairs, into the San Francisco terminal, and hollered, "I am home!"

"Welcome home!" a man hollered back. I turned to see him with a broom in hand, smiling his big smile. I smiled with a thumbs up motion and continued to walk down to baggage claim.

"It's good to be home," I said to Lina.

We gathered up our luggage containing months of stuff, and I walked over to a phone booth to call Father and Mother. The coins clinked as each one dropped into the coin reservoir. The telephone rang across the bay and into the kitchen of the ticky-tacky home I grew up in. The phone rang and rang. Finally, the distant sound of my Father answered, "Hello?"

"It's me, Father. It's Tess. Lina and I are here... at the San Francisco Airport... can you come pick us up?" I said.

"On my way," Father said in a very sleepy voice. "Mother and I will be there in an hour."

Lina sat outside on a nearby bench. I took in a deep breath, closed my eyes and inhaled the salty air. I heard seagulls and airplanes and felt the cold breeze of the San Francisco fog beginning to form. As I sauntered to take a seat next to Lina, I admired our luggage as it sat perfectly lined up on the curb.

CHAPTER 43

J was blinded by the oncoming headlights. I squinted my eyes and stood when I recognized my father's Buick approaching. I rocked back and forth and began jumping up and down, waving and shouting, "Over here!" The vehicle slowed to a stop and Father jumped out of the car, pulling me into an embrace. I felt as though I had been gone forever, and it was so comforting to be in his arms again. Mother sat patiently in the car. I motioned for her to get out. I introduced Lina to Father, and I gave Mother a long-awaited hug. Lina got in the back seat, and I took the center seat between Father and Mother. I had so much to tell them.

We made our journey across the San Mateo Bridge to San Leandro, and I talked non-stop. What usually took about 25 minutes to travel, seemed to be over in a matter of minutes. I talked, and talked, and talked so much that I put Lina to sleep. It never occurred to me that my parents were up in the middle of the night, and they needed to work in a few hours. My body had so much adrenaline passing through it, I had no concept of time.

"What happened to our home?" I asked as we pulled into our ticky-tacky drive way. It looked way different, and Father explained how he changed our home into a duplex. The west side of our home had been transformed into a two-bedroom unit. My bedroom was no longer mine, and my parents were living on the east side with two remaining bedrooms. The front entrance was no longer ours. We walked around to the back entrance. As we entered, I looked around and asked, "Where are all my things?"

Mother just laughed, "Oh, we gave them to the Salvation Army." My bedroom furniture was gone, my shoes, my clothes, and all my years of memorabilia from countless Raiders' and Oakland A's games. Reality set in, and I fathomed that my adult life had officially begun.

I looked down at my luggage containing all my worldly possessions. I teared up, but refused to let my parents see my reaction. I smiled and politely said, "Cool."

With an added weight, I sat down on the couch and looked up at Lina, "You take the guest room, I will sleep on the couch."

I couldn't sleep. I stared at my opened suitcases and hoped that I had enough clothes to hold me over for a while. I needed a job, and I needed it right away. I walked over and picked up my parent's telephone to call Elio. I did not consider the hour; I needed to hear his voice. I waited in anticipation as the phone rang, once, then twice. It continued to ring over and over again, so I hung up and let out a sigh.

The sound of the coffee perking and music in the bathroom woke me from a brief sleep. Father and Mother were ready for work. My father appeared and leaned over me, requesting that I drive them in. Evidently, my car was gone as well. I got up and quickly took a very short Colombian style shower. I whispered to Lina, "I'll be back, you just sleep while I drive my parents into work."

The sound of our small community seemed so quiet compared to only yesterday. As I drove my parents Buick, I braved the question, "What happened to my car? Did you sell it?"

"No, it is getting paint and bodywork. I was going to surprise you, Tess," my Father reassured me. That was a huge relief, and I smiled while merging north onto the Nimitz freeway. It was early morning, and the sun was just making its way over the bay. I thought about Elio and wondered why he did not answer his phone? We arrived in Jack London Square, downtown Oakland. I admired the harbor containing rows and rows of boats. "Pick us up at six," my father instructed me as they exited their car.

I smiled, blew them a kiss, turned on the radio, and hit the gas pedal. I briefly felt free again.

As I approached my turn off to San Leandro, I passed it by. I continued south on the Nimitz freeway to Hayward. I will pay Elio a surprise visit. My mind raced, and my heart beat like a drum. I turned up the volume on the radio to hear Leon Russell sing "A song for you." My foot became heavier and heavier on the gas pedal. I swiftly made my exit off the freeway and traveled up the winding road to his home.

I slowed to a stop in front of Elio's house and stared at the glowing porch light. The drapes were closed, giving the impression that no one was home. I sat in my car and stared, and from the recesses of my mind, I heard voices echoing.

I heard voices of disappointment; I saw memories of fading headlights; I saw rows and rows of walnut orchards, and I saw luggage sitting neatly on the curb at the airport. I saw the eyes of a man on a bus, and I heard the laughter of a poor child begging me to stay. I saw the dark kitchen with cold food on my plate. I heard a phone ring and ring and ring.

My throat tightened up. It was difficult to swallow. The tears welled up in my eyes. I sensed that something was wrong. I glanced up at the porch one more time and soaked up the raspy voice of Leon Russell. I moved the gear shift arm into drive, released my brake, and slowly drifted away. I looked around the familiar streets, smelled the familiar air, and heard sounds of early morning traffic. Elio's words rang in my ears, "I will be here when you return"; sea sponge in hand. I gazed at my hands on the steering wheel and drove the long way home.

CHAPTER 44

I entered my parent's back door with the exhaustion and disappointment firmly set in. Nothing was what I expected. I threw the car keys on the kitchen counter, took off my shoes and plopped on the couch. The old familiar coo-coo clock sounded, and then the mantle clock answered. I allowed my memory to drift back to my sister's wedding, and Derk.

THE HONKING OF A HORN OUTSIDE STARTLED ME, AND I LOOKED OUT MY living room window as a car passed by. For hours I waited for Derk to pick me up. My sister Angie got married earlier that day, and my date appeared to have stood me up. My family was in the city checking out the hippies on Height and Ashbury Streets. We had such a good day, and I was wondering what happened? Another car passed by without stopping.

I decided not to sit around for anyone. I picked up the phone to call my girlfriend Yvette. "Hey Yvette, it's Tess, do you want to go to an engagement party?" She said she was willing, so I drove over and picked her up. We made our way to Arthur and Louisa's party. It was a light blue ticky-tacky home in the Manor, very close to the park. We made small talk with many friends as we forged our way into the heart of the home. I saw Louisa talking to a guest when I approached to congratulate her and her fiancé. Louisa thanked me with her big friendly smile, flashing her big ring. She gave me a hug. She then tapped a man on his shoulder. He turned, and she introduced him as her fiancé, Arthur. He was a striking man, blonde with beautiful green eyes, and a great sun tan. He smiled a big smile and shook my hand. "Hello," I said.

"Hello," he repeated with a chuckle. "Have a glass of champagne," he said as he grabbed a glass and poured.

"Thank you," I said and turned to walk away.

Yvette poked me in the back and pointed to the front walkway. I saw my date, Derk, walking up with another woman. My mouth dropped open, and I set my champagne down, making my way out the front door. Derk was surprised to see me, and the look on my face spoke volumes. He stopped, and his date disappeared. I grabbed him by the arm and yanked him away from the party.

"How could you stand me up and then show up with another woman?" I hollered. He stopped walking and looked down at me and said, nothing. "What a fool I am. We are over, way over," I said, and then I turned and walked back to my car. Yvette was watching us and met me at the car. We both jumped in, I started the car, pushed down the clutch, and slipped the gearshift into first gear. I glanced over at the party and noticed Arthur standing on the porch. Our eyes met, and he watched as my car drove down the street and out of sight.

A few months later, the honking sounds of the geese flying over my ticky-tacky home in the Manor, caught my attention as I sat on the front porch of my home. I imagined flying away with them and then looked down at my feet. I sat, uncertain about my next move. *Derk the Jerk! Andre would never have stood me up.* It was a beautiful day as fall set in, and the leaves changed to orange and red. I thought of taking a drive over to Tower Records. It was my day off from the hospital, and Diana Ross has a new album out.

I jumped in my 58 Karman Ghia, turned up my radio, and rolled down my windows. I drove into the parking lot of the local Tower Records store and noticed a black Porsche heading my way. I turned down my radio and slowed to a stop alongside him. Elio's car window slowly rolled down.

~

THE RINGING PHONE WOKE ME FROM MY SLUMBER ON THE COUCH OF MY parent's home. I looked around the living room, and rose to answer it. A strange familiar voice on the other end chills me to my core, "Hello Tess, Welcome Home." I immediately hung up the phone, and wondered how *he* knew I was home?

I tried to imagine who my caller was? Could it have been my neighbor, or perhaps the man who cornered me on the dark street one night? He seemed to know my every move. My senses were confused and yet, I clung to the idea that love would prevail.

I was suddenly hungry, and I craved an American hamburger. Not just a hamburger, I craved an American cheeseburger, with French fries and catsup. I smiled at the thought of seeking comfort from something I could sink my teeth into. I walked over to my parent's guest room, and found Lina fast asleep. "Are you hungry, I whisper?"

"No," she murmured. "I just want to sleep."

The closest McDonalds was in Hayward, and it just so happened to be a walking distance from Elio's hair salon; The Monte Carlo. I cleaned myself up, and drove to McDonalds and ordered a Big Mac with French fries.

As I sat in my father's Buick, consuming the best burger in the entire world, I noticed Elio's black Porsche parked nearby. I finished eating and with hesitation, walked over to the salon. Elio was in the front window cutting someone's hair. I stopped and waited for him to look my way, and when he did, I waved. He smiled back and motioned for me to come in.

In what seemed like a movie in slow motion, I entered the salon and we hugged. "I am home," I announced.

"Let's go to dinner," Elio said, "What about Saturday night?"

"Perfect" I responded, "I look forward to seeing you."

My heart beat with anticipation as I popped into Tower Records to purchase a new album. I casually entered the showcase of hundreds of recordings, and selected one of the albums on display; "The Main Ingredient." It seemed just right.

CHAPTER 45

*I*t was a busy Saturday at the airport. I looked over my shoulder and watched people feverishly walk to catch flights to their planned destinations. Lina and I sat at her assigned gate in the San Francisco Airport. We enjoyed a few days in the bay area, and Father and Mother were happy to get to know her. We dined the night before at the Pinecone Restaurant in San Leandro, my mother's favorite. Lina was excited to get back to Seattle and reunite with her husband. I was sad to see her go; I was equally excited to meet up with Elio that night for our dinner.

Lina's flight was called over the loudspeaker system, prompting Lina to stand. "Love you Lina" I said, as she picked up her carry-on bag. "Come see me in Seattle!" Lina said, as we embraced.

I watched as she stopped to present her boarding pass, and then she walked through the double doors and down the breeze-way. Memories of my recent walks down endless breeze-ways, numerous airports, and sitting in assigned seats waiting for the announcement, "Fasten your seat belts" thrust in. I imagined my "cocaine flight attendant" hard at work, and then I looked around, and noticed the gate was empty. "Time to go home," I said to myself.

A long breath exited my mouth, and the thought of Elio's eyes made my feet move faster. Just like that, and before I knew it, I was running out of the airport to my father's Buick.

It was a lovely morning as I drove across the San Mateo Bridge. A slight haze captured the horizon as the tide moved in. The shape of the Salt Mines reminded me of "Sugar Loaf" in Rio de Janeiro. I turned up the radio and relished the moment. *I will have to find a job very soon and I cannot wait too long.*

I rummaged through my suitcase, and found my custom-made black long-sleeve sweater, and my custom-made black bell bottoms. I slipped on my black suede platform dress-shoes, and my custom-made black rain coat. My long hair was braided down one side behind my ear, showing off my Brazilian earrings that Mamai gave me. I added the matching necklace and ring. I finished my look with a spray of the Chanel perfume that Reeta purchased for me. I smiled when I realized I had a bit of everyone with me this evening.

The door-bell rang, and I ran to my parent's back door. I opened the door to Elio. Beautiful Elio. I composed myself this time, and I stood on my tiptoes to kiss his cheek, Brazilian style. I closed the door behind me, and we left hand in hand. Elio led me to a big black Cadillac parked outside. I was puzzled and looked to Elio questioning, "Where is your Porsche?"

"We are going to dinner with some friends," he said. He opened the door to the back seat, and I slid in.

"Hello," I greeted the couple in the front seat.

"Hello", they replied. "How's the world traveler?"

"I am fantastic," I said, and Elio introduced me to Ron and Kathy. We drove to San Francisco for dinner, mostly talking about my travels along the way. We arrived at a beautiful new restaurant called the Green Room. Plants hung everywhere, and the sound of flowing water created an outdoor exotic ambiance.

The four of us were seated, and I looked at Elio, "Will you order for me?" I then excused myself to the ladies' room. I was soon followed by Ron's date, Kathy. We freshened up, and Ms. Date Crasher inquired about my time in South America. She asked if I was able to bring back any good cocaine. I was surprised and chose not to hide my look of amazement! "What is it with cocaine?" I asked her.

"There is a lot of good stuff coming out of Colombia, and I thought since you were there. Well, you know," she said.

"Are you a flight attendant?" I asked, and she just stared at me.

After a lovely dinner, we meandered around Fisherman's Wharf, hand in hand. Ron and his date were fun to chat with. We stopped to enjoy numerous street musicians. As we rounded a corner near Ghirardelli Square, I stopped abruptly to admire a street tap dancer. He had a sheet of plywood on the ground and pounded away as Dave Brubeck played "Take Five." I valued his talent and remembered my endless dance classes. A five, six, seven, eight.... rang in my head. "One more time. One more time. One more time," my dance instructor repeated. I smiled at the dancer, and Elio threw some money in his hat placed on the ground. The artist winked and flashed us his brilliant white, toothy smile.

We traveled across the San Francisco Bay, and Elio and I were dropped off at his home in Hayward. Finally, alone. I felt at home among his familiar Andy Warhol collections on the walls and the crushed green velvet couch. I kicked off my platform shoes and ran over to his stereo with The Main Ingredient album I had purchased. Elio lit a fire in the fireplace as I talked, non-stop, about my travels and experiences.

Elio listened patiently, his brown eyes blazing into mine. Elio was color blind, and I wondered what color my eyes were to him? My nervousness settled down from the comforting air he projected. Suddenly, he covered my mouth with his hand. He gently kissed my neck, and lowered me to his gold shag carpet, in front of the crackling fireplace. Soft music played: "I just don't want to be lonely".

Elio's mood-lamp, of yellow and orange, along with my young starry-eyed mind, swirled around and around.

CHAPTER 46

$\mathcal{T}$he hot evening of August 8, 1974, I asked, "Who is our President now?"

We all watched as President Nixon resigned as President of the United States. It was difficult to watch on the small television set in Sao Paulo, Brazil. My Brazilian family and I gathered around the television to watch my president speak. I was confused listening to his voice dubbed in Portuguese, while trying to read the subtitles moving across the bottom of the screen. I remained seated on the edge of the couch, miles away from home, as we watched our twentieth century democracy fall apart before my eyes.

"I have never been a quitter," I read as President Nixon spoke. His official date of resignation was set for August 9, 1974. Vice President Gerald Ford would be sworn in as our 38th President of the United States. My Brazilian friends and family members were constantly asking political questions about America. I would discuss the history of presidents, the historic corruption, the numerous assassinations, shootings targeted at famous artists and musicians, and now we had Watergate.

"H<small>AVE YOU HEARD</small> T<small>ESS, WE HAVE A NEW PRESIDENT,</small>" E<small>LIO HOLLERED</small> from the kitchen. It was early morning, and I slowly opened my eyes. The sun was just starting to peak into the room. Coffee brewed in the kitchen; promising I would be more alert soon. I looked around the bedroom at the clothes scattered about, shoes tossed here and there, and my eyes settled on the boots. Elio appeared with two cups of coffee and placed them right next to his bed. "Good morning," he said as he leaped onto the bed and kissed me. "Did you hear about Watergate?"

"Yes, I watched it on TV in Brazil," I said. "I need to go home soon, I should call my father and let him know I am here, he must be worried. May I use your phone?"

"What did you make of it?" Elio asked. I walked over to the phone, ignoring his inquiry, and called home. My Father answered, and I explained that I was with Elio and would be home later. I apologized for not calling sooner and explained that I had fallen asleep. "Thanks for calling Tess, you are an adult now and there's no need to explain, but I appreciate that you did," he said. As I hung up the phone, I notice a puzzled look on Elio's face. It was a look that I had not seen before. He seemed to be very far away in thought.

"I have a gift for you Elio," I said. I pulled out of my purse the Italian pipe that Papai bought for me. "It was a gift from my Brazilian Father, and I want you to have it. When Papai and I would smoke after dinner, I would think of you. I know how much you enjoy smoking a pipe," I said with a smile. Elio thanked me with his soft whisper. We settled into a morning of fun conversation. I wanted to hear more about his time while I was away. He seemed reluctant to share, but I continued to push him until he finally confessed.

"I have met another woman," he said, "She is closer to my age and successful with her own business. I feel we have so much in common, Tess, especially since I have my own salon now." As I sat looking into his eyes, I saw the conflict. I remembered this conflict in me before leaving, and now the tides had turned.

"Well, then," I said, "Perhaps you should continue to see this woman so you can be sure of who and what you want."

"How can you be so understanding?" Elio asked.

"Because I am young, and I will wait because, because (I hesitate to say the truth) because I want to be the most important person; to someone. I *do not* want to be a consolation prize for anyone. Life is complicated enough, Elio, and I need to find a job."

I had fumbled over my words. After hearing them out loud, it was obvious to me, just how dumb I had sounded and how young I was, compared to her. I had nothing, and she had everything, it seemed, even him.

I remembered one of our many dates. Our evening began with the viewing of "The Way We Were" starring Robert Redford and Barbara Streisand, ending with a casual drive down East 14th Street. Elio leaned over and said to me, "You know Tess, I realized back when I received my driver's license, you were just a newborn baby. However, when I am 116 years old, you will only be 100, and that does not sound so bad." We both laughed.

It was not so funny now as I looked again to Elio for some comfort, some reassurance, but most of all I looked to him for love. I watched as he paced back and forth across the living room floor, before putting on his leather jacket and cowboy boots. He started to say something and then stopped. He looked at me and shook his head, opened his mouth to speak and then sighed. My senses had seized the torment inside of him.

I feared that he judged me as a Daddy's girl without a career, a job, or a home. Elio struggled with our age difference. I could tell he worried that I would get bored with him. Maybe he worried that he would hold me back from not sure what. I was small and fragile in his eyes, and I was just starting out in life. I saw him as my strength, my comfort, and my safety net, though I did not say the words. I was silent and said nothing.

Elio drove me back to my parents' home that morning. It was a quiet drive, and I tried to switch gears in my head. I looked at the fine midst on the windshield, the remnants of light showers on the streets, and *thought not of the past, but of the future.*

What could I do now? Then I remembered President Nixon. Those were the *exact words* he said when he left the Oval Office.

CHAPTER 47

*T*he winds aloft had shifted, and I looked up at my reflection in the bathroom mirror. My hair was a mess, my eyes were black from the mascara running down my face. I felt that life was not worth living. I stared down at the prescription pills that I emptied into my hand. They made me feel sleepy when I took only one, as prescribed. I pondered what would happen if I took them all? I filled my drinking glass full of water and took another look down at the pills. I looked into the eyes of my reflection, inhaled slowly through my nose, and exhaled through my pursed lips. Without further hesitation, I tossed the pills into my mouth, and took a big gulp of water. I looked up and into the mirror beyond my reflection. Remorse immediately set in. I asked myself over and over, "What have I done?"

I quietly tiptoed into the master bedroom where my husband laid sleeping. I slid into bed alongside him and quietly listened to his breathing while he slept unaware. My mind raced with thoughts of dying, wondering if I really wanted to die? Is he worth it?

I leaned over and nudged him. "Wake up, wake up Arthur!" Arthur sat up looking agitated at me with his *do not-bother-me* look. "I have done something and now, I don't, I don't know?" I said.

"What did you do?" he asked, and I just laid there.

My voice cracked in fear and I found it difficult to speak.

"What did you do?" he repeated.

I blurted out, "I took all my prescription pills, the ones that make me drowsy."

Arthur jolted out of bed and headed for the telephone. He called the local hospital emergency room and spoke with the physician on duty. He dropped the phone and ran to grab the empty bottle from the bathroom. He returned to the phone and continued talking to the physician. I laid in bed, listening to the one-sided conversation. I wondered, what will happen and how long will it take?

I visualized the pills dissolving one by one, and the lining of my stomach absorbing the toxins as he spoke in slow motion. Time stood still, just as the jet lumbered over the breaks of water coming into San Francisco. I could almost touch the waves.

Arthur hung up the receiver and looked through our refrigerator. He came into our room and grabbed me by the arm. He dragged me into the bathroom and shoved his hand down my throat. "You need to throw up!" he screamed at me. "Throw up now!" he continued pounding on my back. He repeated his words and tried gagging me. His fingers were large and his grip strong. I cried hysterically. I couldn't throw up. "Do it yourself Tess, try to throw up!" Arthur continued his ranting and raving. "How many did you take? I need to run to the store, we need mustard. The doctor said to have you drink warm water with mustard, and that will cause you to regurgitate!"

I laid on the floor in silence. Mustard? Arthur threw on his clothes and dashed out the door. I embraced the stillness. My mascara caked eyes stung, and I fought to open them. My nose ran profusely, and my body shook. I tried to make myself throw up, but I could never do it. Panic set in, and I feared Arthur would not return.

My mind played tricks on me, and I felt myself slipping into a dream state. I imagined Arthur coming home the next day. He had the perfect alibi; he wasn't home. The police would determine that I committed suicide and Arthur would be free of me. But wait, I remembered that he called the hospital. I drifted in and out of consciousness, and I waited for his return. I stared at the ceiling, and I remembered my father, my daddy who sang to me as a child. I heard boxes, little boxes, and then I heard the familiar sound of a Harley Davidson nearby. The tips of my fingers twitched in rhythm to the notes.

I saw my grandfather and heard his voice shouting at me, "Move Tess, move about," as I laid motionless.

The entry door slammed shut, and I heard Arthur approach the bathroom. He had a glass of warm mustard water and lifted me up to drink. "Drink this Tess, drink it all," Arthur ordered. I drank the nasty concoction, but I did not vomit. Arthur called the hospital a second time and spoke to the physician again. He hung up the phone and returned to the bathroom with a second glass of mustard water. "Drink it again," he said. I drank and still no vomiting. I continued crying hysterically. Arthur looked at me as I laid on the floor and curled into a fetal position. He ran his hands through his blonde hair, his green eyes lit in fiery anger, and he shook his head. "Go to bed Tess," he said. "You are not going to die," and he turned and walked away.

I slowly stood and stared at the reflection in the mirror. I saw someone else, someone I had never met. I washed my face, hoping to be someone I could recognize. I could barely swallow and my throat throbbed in pain. My eyes were swollen to a small squint. I glanced towards our bedroom and heard Arthur snoring. I felt ashamed and sheepishly walked into *my own darkness.*

Slipping back into bed, I remained deep in thought. *What if Arthur said I was not going to die, because he hoped I would?* I fought to keep my eyes open and struggled with the urge to fall asleep. I continued wondering how I came to marry this man? Arthur and I fought all the time.

It was Sunday night, and I was supposed to go to work soon. Morning approached, and *thoughts of leaving* ran through my drug-infested foggy brain. I saw beautiful puffy clouds in the sky, and on the bathroom walls of my past. I hated Arthur. I saw myself running down a sandy path that led to a can of Campbell's tomato soup, and then I fell fast asleep.

CHAPTER 48

*I*t was a typical Saturday night, and I called my dear friend Yvette. "Do you want to go to the drive-in movies?" I asked her.

"Of-course I do, Tess!" Yvette said. Yvette and I were always there for our; nothing to do nights. We had been friends since grammar school.

I remembered the day we met; Yvette rode up on a *too-big-for-her* bicycle to the front of my ticky-tacky home in the Manor. She was new in the neighborhood, and I was in the sixth year at school. "Do you want to play?" she asked. I looked at her and wondered, "Who asks that kind of question at our age?" I gave her my older sister Katie's big sister look. You know, the one that looks you up and down, and then there's a rise of the right side of the upper lip.

"I am busy, I am going to a gymnastic event at school," I replied to her. I had signed up for the event and was on my way. I think she thought I was making it up, but I was not.

We eventually became friends in junior high school. Our circle of friends came together, and I found myself hanging out at her house more and more. Yvette had one older brother, who was only referred to as "brother", and her parents referred to me as "dimples". Our relationship became a love affair of two families that were complete opposites. We did have one thing in common. We both moved into the Manor from Oakland.

"What movie are we going to see Tess?" Yvette asked as I picked her up in my Father's White Cloud. "Who cares, let's just see what's playing," I said, as we drove over to the Bay-fair Drive-In, double movie screen complex.

We decided on *Woodstock* the documentary about the famous music concert held August 16, 1969, outside of New York City. We pulled up alongside the double speaker. I positioned the speaker in the window, just right, and rolled it up. I adjusted the volume as we sat back to enjoy the movie. Yvette and I were laughing at the preliminary cartoons, when a silver step-side Chevy pickup slowly parked alongside us. The occupants rolled down their window, and Yvette recognized the driver. She rolled her window down and began talking with two guys in the truck. I leaned over, and it was my turn to recognize the driver. It was Arthur from the engagement party we attended. I smiled and said hello as Arthur and his friend, George, got out of their truck. Yvette invited them to sit in the back seat of my father's car, and before I knew it, we were a party of four. "Hello Arthur," I said, "How is Louisa?"

"We broke off our engagement," he said.

"I am sorry to hear that. Hello George," I said. We chatted about this and that, and we never watched *Woodstock*. However, good music played in the background, as the guys passed around a joint.

I WOKE TO THE TELEPHONE RINGING OVER AND OVER. I LOOKED OVER AT my empty bed and walked over to the phone. "Where are you Tess? Are you okay?"

I looked at the clock on the kitchen wall and noticed I was late for work. "Yes, I am ok, thank you," I struggled to speak. "I am obviously late this morning. I was up sick all night. I am so sorry for not calling, I must have fallen back to sleep." As I hung up the phone, I looked around our small duplex and noticed I was alone. I walked into the bathroom and gazed at my almost recognizable reflection. My eyes were still swollen, and I looked like someone punched my face multiple times. I relived Arthur's actions as he smacked me around and beat me on the back. I dropped my robe to the floor to check out the bruises on my body. I turned on the shower, allowing the hot water to run down my head. I felt nothing.

I drove to Levine Hospital in Hayward. I worried how I looked as I headed to the Radiology department. I parked my 58 Karmann Ghia and made the long walk to the E.R. and X-ray entrance. It was noon; I was very late for work. I attempted to seem nonchalant when I entered the department. The technicians on duty stared. I looked down and walked in with no words and punched my time card in the time clock. I told anyone that asked, that I was sick with a flu. My coworkers continued skeptically, looking me over. Or at least it felt like they were. The phone rang at my desk, and I answered to Arthur's voice. "How are you feeling, Tess?" he asked me.

"I am okay," I murmured.

"You know, Tess, I could have taken you to the hospital and they would have put you under psychiatric evaluation," Arthur said. "You are lucky I did not do that," he added.

"Thank you," I said, and I hung up the phone.

I was riddled with embarrassment, and I wanted no one to know, but instead, my co-workers dragged me off to lunch. "I just arrived!" my voice cracked. My throat ached. That didn't stop them from packing me into a car.

On our way to lunch they asked, "What happened to you?" I sat in stillness and bewilderment, unable to find the right words.

We drove to a local Mexican restaurant in silence. I looked over at Morgan, who was driving, and I realized what good people I worked with. Morgan was black, Bettina was Italian, Juan was Mexican, Caleb was a Jewish guy with a big afro hairstyle, and then there was me. A white girl, part British, Irish, German, young and naïve, and I was unable to convince anyone in this car that I had the flu.

CHAPTER 49

*A*rthur and I began dating in the winter of 1975. He was charming, handsome, and very popular within our social circle. Arthur's immediate family lived in San Lorenzo, a town that sat right alongside mine. Arthur was five years older than me, and after the night at the drive in, we spent every minute with each other. Arthur had two roommates, Stan and Kevin, and they all lived in Hayward. We spent most of our time snow skiing in the winter, water skiing in the summer, camping with friends at Pinecrest Resort, dining out, and catching good movies.

It was never a dull moment with Arthur. He was close friends with a new band that formed, called Yesterday and Today. We would drive into San Francisco and watch them perform at small pubs and venues. They rocked in the 70s and became pretty well known. We watched them open at the Cow Palace for New Year's Eve. Arthur and I had backstage passes. We mingled with the bands, but I remained quiet and reserved.

It was spring of 1976, when Arthur asked me to marry him. "Yes!" I responded without hesitation. I was not expecting a proposal. Arthur slipped a beautiful diamond ring on my finger. We were at our favorite restaurant, The Hungry Hunter. I smiled as my inquisitive mind stared at my engagement ring.

"Let's get married in June," Arthur said.

"June?" I said, mesmerized by the beautiful sparkle on my finger. I looked up at my soon to be husband. I responded with a slight hesitation, "Yes, June it is," and we kissed.

Arthur and I spent weeks planning and putting together our special day. I selected a beautiful venue in Castro Valley, the Willow Park Country Club. I walked the grounds with Arthur as we toured the outdoor gazebo chosen for our ceremony. Stan offered to be our photographer, and from our local Salvation Army Church, Captain Reed accepted the invitation to perform the ceremony.

June 13, 1976, was a warm sunny day. I was chauffeured by my father and mother. We pulled up in front of the main building, in the white cloud. My mother carried my gown, and my father carried my suitcase. I borrowed my sister Angie's wedding gown, and after many alterations, it was a perfect dress. It was white satin, with many small beads sewn around the bodice. As I dressed, my sister Angie adjusted my veil, and Father helped with my shoes.

Our ceremony began with two talented young men singing; Loggins & Messina's "The Love Song." I walked the long walk, Father in hand, into Arthur's waiting arms. As we stood before all, I heard the voice of Captain Reed reciting our vows, while golf balls flew by our gazebo aimed at the ninth hole. The birds sang in the trees, and an occasional, "Fore," set the romantic tone for our day. I often wondered if I was making the right decision?

Our guests were attended to in the banquet room, and we selected Post Raisin Band to entertain at the reception. The band played, and the room lit up with voices and laughter as guests made their way to the dance floor. Arthur and I had our first dance as man and wife. I gazed at the band as their lead singer, Tommy, belted out a Tower of Power song, "You're Still a Young Man." I remembered Fred Abrams, and my time at band camp. I danced in Arthur's embrace, and my thoughts turned to Elio. Elio had become far from my reach. I quickly dismissed him and nestled my face into Arthur's shoulder. Arthur was wearing a white tux, white shirt and white shoes. I was 20 years old, married, and my life with Arthur was all that mattered.

~

MY COWORKERS CONTINUED TO PRESS ME. I FINALLY BROKE DOWN AND spilled the events of the prior night. They sat in silence and occasionally munched on Mexican food. My voice cracked and my lower lip quivered as I reached up to wipe the moisture around my eyes. My dear friends from work announced they were all going to attend a musical production in San Francisco Saturday night! I looked up at them and modestly smiled. "I have never been to a musical before!" They had an extra ticket for *Annie,* and we are all going to Benihana's for dinner, before the performance. I was suddenly filled with hope, and the thought of being with people who cared about me warmed my heart. "Ok, then it looks like I have a date this Saturday night!" I exclaimed.

I stared out the car window on our way back to work. Juan leaned over and whispered in my ear, "Leave him Tess, you deserve better. I would never hurt you." I looked into the eyes of my co-worker and friend. I looked back out of the window.

A bird flew along-side the car, flapping his wings to keep up with us, and then my eyes focused on a small airplane in the distance. I remembered flying with my Father and I wondered, will I ever fly again?

CHAPTER 50

*B*irds flew over me as I ran the sandy path of the San Leandro Marina. I took in the salty air and found my usual seat on the park bench, watching the jets land in Oakland.

Arthur and I had been married for six months, and he wanted to watch a local band play at a nearby pub that night. It was a hit and miss when we would go out. Sometimes, I would get carded at the door, when we tried to enter a venue serving alcohol. If I was questioned, we were asked to leave. I was not yet 21 years of age.

Nervousness set in as we approached the entry of Lucky Lions in the Oakland Hills. Arthur became agitated with me and told me to relax. I stood just slightly behind Arthur, when he approached the door-man to pay our cover fee. I felt my body tense up, and his grip became tighter and tighter.

We were allowed in, and I relaxed a bit when I watched the band set up. "The lead guitarist is from the Manor," Arthur whispered in my ear. I looked at the musicians, and I noticed a tall dark man with long wavy brown hair. His hair hung halfway down his back and chest, and he had a large wooly mustache. His eyes were intense, dark, and rested just beneath his thick dark eyebrows. He never smiled. He looked scary to me.

We were seated at a small cocktail table. More of my high school friends arrived, and it seemed that everyone I knew came to see the local band. When I saw Yvette, I got up to visit with her. "Who is the lead guitarist?" I asked.

"Carlos Romero," she told me. I looked up at him, and I remembered. I remembered him from my childhood. He had changed dramatically, and I would not have recognized him, had Yvette not told me who he was.

I took my seat along-side my husband, when the band began their set. Carlos wore very tight gold pants. His guitar sat against his abdomen as he electrified the audience with his talented fingers. His tight gold pants held my attention. Everything this man was not endowed with was perfectly displayed just below his guitar. My pupils enlarged, and my mouth dropped open. How did he not know? I asked myself. Arthur and I sat comfortably at a small cocktail table, and I found myself staring at a very small cock. A cigarette hung from Arthur's mouth as he winked at me. Then he began to laugh.

Arthur pulled into our drive-way, and we walked into our small duplex. It was late, and Arthur had been drinking way too much. He pulled a nicely folded rectangle piece of paper out of his pocket. He opened it and laid out a big white line of cocaine on our kitchen counter. "How about we enjoy this Tess?" he asked. I looked at the powder, shook my head indicating that I would pass. Arthur laughed and pulled a dollar bill out of his wallet, rolling it up into the shape of a straw. He leaned over and snorted the white line. "Nice," he said and smiled at me. I dropped my purse on the counter and proceeded to get ready for bed.

Arthur appeared at our bedroom doorway and announced he wanted to go out and see some friends. "I'll be home later," he said. Arthur grabbed the car keys and drove down the street. I dropped onto the bed and lay there staring at the ceiling. It dawned on me, I was married to a drug addict, and I felt very alone again.

～

As I sat at the Marina, I wondered what can I do? *I must make my marriage work; I cannot give up so easily.* I reflected on that night, as I ran back down the path to my car. I planned to prepare a nice dinner. Christmas was next week, and we didn't have a Christmas tree.

Money was tight. It was a miserable thought, and I continued running. I admired the decorated street lamps adorned in Christmas garland, with a gold bell tied in the center. Across the way, I noticed a Salvation Army Officer next to his Christmas kettle, ringing his bell. The vision was all too clear.

~

My sisters and I had stood next to a red kettle, singing Christmas carols at the local mall. Captain Smith stood waving his band leader hand as the brass band played alongside us. We were so young, and I noticed a group of teenage boys approaching. They were smoking cigarettes and looked a lot like my oldest brother, and James Dean. They laughed at us. I was confused why they would laugh. Then they pitched pennies at us. I leaned over to pick them up. After all, I was from a poor family and when I saw a penny; I knew that could buy candy and gum.

Captain Smith squeezed my shoulder, and I looked up at him. He waved his finger at me, while shaking his head no. I stopped and continued singing while the young men continued laughing. I felt embarrassed. I could hear the laughter of the young men as I ran away in my saddle shoes. Their laughter faded, along with the ringing of the bell.

~

I jumped in my Karmann Ghia and drove over to a Christmas tree lot on East 14th street. I purchased a small 2-foot tree, threw it in my back seat, and headed home. "Chin up," I told myself, "It can always be worse." I pulled into our duplex and the empty driveway. I made my way into our home and set up the Christmas tree on a small end table.

I scrambled through the recipe box and found my recipe for Christmas ornaments. I opened a kitchen drawer and pulled out my cookie cutters in shapes of Christmas trees, Santa Claus, stars, and camels. I baked the ornaments and as they cooled, I punched a small hole in their top side and drew a small thread through its opening. I found my paintbrush and paint set from high school and painted them. It turned into a fun project, and I beamed as I hung them one by one on our first Christmas tree.

The tree brightened the atmosphere in the bleak little box we called our home, and I hoped it would bring a smile to Arthur's face when he arrived. I had no idea where he had gone, probably a bar or a friend's home, so I began preparing our dinner. I set the table for two and waited. I waited as our meal on the stove grew cold. I waited as our room faded into darkness. I lit candles around the living room and picked out a record to play. I turned up the volume and listened to George Benson's, "The Masquerade." I wished I had lights for the tree, but I could not afford them. I turned on the porch light and stood in the doorway looking out. Still no Arthur.

As I put our dinner in the refrigerator, I reminisced about being at home in Brazil, being at home in Colombia, being at home with Father and Mother, smoking a pipe with Papai, and then I looked at the photos on the wall of my wedding day. We looked so happy in the photographs. Photographs reminded me of *National Geographic* magazines. And *National Geographic* magazines reminded me of prison. Prison reminded me of Father, and then I thought of that little boy in the Amazon; Douglas.

I stared beyond the photos on the walls. Thoughts of leaving flowed through my mind as I listened to Benson's smooth voice. I closed my eyes and thought of Elio's brown eyes and the moles that sat below each one. "Just go to bed," I told myself, "It is cold, and I am sure it is snowing, somewhere."

My eyes scanned the tiny branches of our Christmas tree; I made sure the ornaments were perfectly presented. I realized; it was the only sense that I could control.

CHAPTER 51

*G*rowing up in the Manor seemed to bring unwanted reputation statuses. My sisters and I had the reputation of being the *fertile* sisters.

My oldest sister, Katie, had two children and named her first-born Becky and her second Michael. Katie married her high school sweetheart, Ace, and they purchased a home in Livermore, California.

My second to the oldest sister, Angie, after marrying Mel, gave birth to a son just before Arthur and I were married. His name was Paul.

My third to the oldest sister, Jessica, married while I was in Brazil. It was another shot-gun wedding (Katie's preceded hers). Jessica and her husband, Jacob, welcomed in their son J.J., shortly after my return from South America. My sisters had been very busy, and somehow, I was thrown into the mix with them.

As I observed my sisters getting married, having children, and living happily ever after, I struggled to keep my marriage to Arthur appearing to be a successful one. The thought of having a child was the last thing on my mind, with good reason. Thank goodness for the pill. I was the perfect aunt, and a convenient babysitter. My nephews and nieces loved visiting and staying with me. I gladly accepted when

I was offered the task. Arthur and I had grown apart, and I found myself alone more than not. The children gave me purpose, and I spent my time finding fun things for us to do.

I was with my niece and nephew, Becky and Michael, when we took a day to visit our local zoo. We drove to the Oakland Hills in my bright orange Karmann Ghia. The impressive entrance happily welcomed us. The first exhibit we came to was a large cage with monkeys swinging back and forth from tree branch to tree branch. Becky and Michael stood in awe as they held tightly to me. The children giggled as I pointed out the different monkeys jumping about. While the monkeys all swung around, my eyes were drawn to the walls and barricades preventing them from escaping.

Suddenly, one monkey approached us and began masturbating. My mouth dropped open as Becky asked, "What is the monkey doing, Aunt Tess?" It took all of two seconds for the monkey to finish, while the monkey and I locked onto each other's eyes. I was appalled, and it sent chills throughout my body. I whisked away my niece and nephew to other exhibits.

I decided I was not a zoo fan. I felt sorry for the animals in the zoo. It was a place of containment and no one likes to be contained, least of all me.

My sibling's children looked up to their Uncle Arthur, for some reason. I think they saw him as a handsome, strong uncle. Arthur worked out at the gym and was very toned. His Australian heritage allowed him to tan easily, and his hair would get very blonde in the summer months.

Arthur was quite the ladies' man, and it seemed all the ladies, except me, drooled over him. Arthur made a habit of going out every Saturday night with his younger single brother, Nate. A small detail in Arthur's mind, but a big detail in mine.

I would gear up before the weekend, knowing Arthur would go out without me. I begged for him to stay home, or suggested we go to the theatre, or maybe I could wait in the car? "Just don't leave me alone," I begged in my pathetic, weepy voice. Arthur would look at me with a smirk on his face and remind me that I was not old enough to go. I saw my father's plane taxi away. I was always too young. Too young to attend my brother's funeral, too young to attend school in Idaho, too young for Elio to love. As I laid on our bed staring at the ceiling, I listened to the sound of the door slamming shut, and I whispered, "But I have my shoes!"

I had turned into a miserable, lonely wife. The phone rang, and I got up off my sorry ass and answered it.

It was my sister Jessica, "Tess, can I bring J.J. over for the night?" she asked.

"Yes, yes, bring him over," I responded.

I hung up the receiver and cleaned myself up. J.J. and Jessica bounced in my door about an hour later. J.J. ran into my arms. He was two years old, and he had the sweetest smile. His lower lip reminded me of a jelly bean, and when he missed his Mom, he stuck out his lower lip and told me, "I want my Mama."

I was so glad that he was there with me. We settled in anticipating a nice evening watching television. I hugged and rocked him, "It's ok J.J., Mama will be back tomorrow."

It wasn't more than a couple of hours that I nestled into a lovely night with J.J., when Arthur abruptly came in through the door. "Hello Uncle Arthur," J.J. said with a smile.

"Hello," I said, and Arthur frowned. It was obvious he was upset.

"I need to talk with you Tess," he said. I motioned that J.J. and I were watching a show on TV, as *he* is sitting on my lap. Arthur walked over and grabbed my arm, pulling me away from J.J. He rolled off my lap and cried. I repeatedly asked, "Can't this wait?"

Arthur acted like he didn't hear me. He pulled me into our kitchen and threw me against the kitchen cabinet. The pain radiated through my thigh. "What is wrong with you?" I asked.

"You cheating bitch!" he yelled as he continued knocking me back and forth. My body flailed about until my legs were kicked from beneath me, and I fell to the floor. My eyes stared at the patterned linoleum. I laid still on my stomach listening to Arthur's rage, "Come on Tess, get up, get up bitch."

I tried to push myself up, when I felt Arthur's foot between my shoulder blades slamming me back against the floor. My mind was racing. I laid helpless, while J.J. cried out from the living room. "Come on Tess, get up," Arthur shouted at me again and again. I froze.

Suddenly a sharp pain shot from my nose, as Arthur smacked my head against the floor. He chuckled.

I saw my uncle at the restaurant in Oakland, his wooden bird's nose bouncing up and down into the glass of water. I could see my aunt hollering, "Order up." Then I saw her praying over me at bedtime. The water rushes out of the faucet and onto my big toe in the claw-foot bathtub. My safe zone is beyond my reach, and then I could taste blood in my mouth. Arthur's foot pushes down against my back, and I laid lifeless.

I heard myself calling out to Father, "Come get me Father, I need to get out of here."

Father wasn't there. My mind felt like it was a spinning movie reel. I felt myself leave my body. I was upstairs in the back room of the picture show, staring at the image of myself on the big screen. I lay helpless on the dark tarmac. The black silhouettes sat watching the screen while a smoky haze danced about the room.

One, two, three, one more time as my fingers fluttered. Monkeys screeched while piloting their 14-bis planes. The reel of film broke and then I realized that I saw a foursome sitting at a kitchen table as the sun rose in the early morning sky.

CHAPTER 52

G randpa George and Grandma Lea were outside working in the garden. I was in Idaho for five weeks and I desperately wanted to call my father. I told myself to make a collect call the first chance that I got. When I finally was alone with the opportunity, I picked up the telephone receiver on the kitchen wall and dialed the operator. "May I help you?" the woman asked. "Yes, I want to make a collect call to my father, his number is 415-357-2052. Please hurry, this is Tess," I instructed her. I impatiently waited for the connection, and suddenly my Grandpa appeared in the kitchen discovering my perfidy. He grabbed the phone out of my hand and hung it up.

"You are not allowed to use the phone, Tess, not without asking my permission!" he told me in his stern tone.

"I am calling my Father, and I am calling him collect, that way you do not have to pay for it," I said.

Grandfather told me that it didn't matter, I was not allowed to use *his* telephone.

I retreated to my bedroom and pulled out some writing paper. I decided that my only chance of getting help was to write my father a letter and beg him to come and get me. I did not want to stay here any longer. "Please, Father, please come get me," I wrote. "I will do all the laundry, ironing, cleaning, anything you ask, just please come save me!"

I snuck an envelope and stamp from my Grandmother's writing table. I woke early the next morning, before anyone was up. I tip-toed out to the rural road my grandparents lived on, and I slipped my letter into the mailbox. I pulled the flag up, hoping the mail carrier's signal to pick up mail didn't alert Grandpa or Grandma. I ran back into the farmhouse and slipped back into bed.

I stared at the bunk bed above me and noticed the pattern of wire holding it in place. The vision became fuzzy as I tried to focus.

GREEN AND YELLOW PATTERNS OF MY LINOLEUM FLOOR APPEARED DIRTY. I will need to wash the blood off the floor soon. I thought about the bunk bed and laid still and quiet. The faint sound of cow bells disappeared under the cries from J.J.

Arthur finally gave up and grabbed his key, walking out the door again.

My body ached as I slowly got up off the floor, and made my way to J.J. He was crying hysterically, and in an attempt to console both of us, I picked him up and held him. "I am so sorry, let's go for a drive." I grabbed my purse, and his overnight bag, and we left.

My beloved Karmann Ghia took me onto the Nimitz freeway heading south. "We are going to some friends tonight, you know them; Don and Dena Williams," I reassured J.J.

He smiled, "I like them."

"I know you do. They are good people," I whispered. We drove the rest of the way in silence.

At the William's, I slowly walked to the front door with J.J. in my arms. Don and Dena were very close to my sister, and we all knew each other from our years at band camp. I rang the doorbell, and Don opened the door. He took one look at me and blurted, "What happened, Tess?"

"I need to leave J.J. with you for the night. He is not safe at my house." Don seemed to understand. He took J.J. from my arms.

"Are you going to be okay?" Don asked.

"Yes, I will be fine. I will call Jessica and let her know J.J. is here, and he is safe. I can't thank you enough. I am so sorry, so sorry," I mumbled.

I turned, walked out and to my car. I glanced up at the home, knowing J.J. is going to be alright. I turned the key to start my car. Silence.

"Shoot, this darn 6-volt system is a pain," I grumbled as I opened the door. Fortunately, or unfortunately? I always planned my parking spaces so that my vehicle was slightly downhill. This happened all too often. I put my left foot on the ground and shoved the car with what strength I had left. Once I was moving at a good pace, I placed my left foot on the clutch, shifted into first gear and then released the clutch. The engine fired up, and I slowly drove away.

I rotated my radio dial until I tuned in Fleetwood Mac playing "Dreams." I glanced in my rear-view mirror, and then at the broken white lines ahead of me, and counted them one by one.

THE PHONE RANG ONCE, TWICE, AND I LAID STILL ON MY BED AND counted the third ring. I heard Grandpa George answer the phone and then call me into the kitchen. The phone was for me. "It's your Dad," Grandpa scolded. I slowly moved the phone receiver to my ear.

I heard father spout, "Just say yes or no, Tess. Do not say anything else. Listen to my questions, then answer me, Tess. Do you understand?"

"Yes," I respond.

My Father asked me, "Do you want to come home?"

"Yes," I said.

"Do you want me to drive there tomorrow after work, I can be there by Saturday morning?" he said.

"Yes," I responded.

"Ok, let me talk to my father," he said. I handed the phone to my Grandpa and listened as he spoke briefly and briskly with my father. My Grandpa hung up the phone, turned, and faced me with his hands on his hips. His eye glasses were mounted slightly on the tip of his nose, as he looked over their frame at me. He then methodically walked over and sat in his easy chair. My Grandma Lea waited in anticipation, until he finally spoke, "You need to call your dad back, and tell him everything is fine here. Tell him. Tess, he does not need to make that long drive to get you. Your dad works long hours, and the drive is too much for him. Tess, you are being selfish by asking this of your dad. Please call and tell him this. Call him now!"

I looked at my Grandpa and my Grandma cautiously. I decidedly stood up, very straight and ambled toward the hallway. I cocked my head and idiomatically responded, "No, I will not." I walked into my bedroom and closed the door.

I PULLED INTO THE DRIVE-WAY OF MY SMALL, TICKY-TACKY DUPLEX. I sat silently staring at the house and finally, slowly got out and closed the door. It was dark. A chill blew in the air across the back of my neck and down my spine. The sounds of cars driving down the Boulevard faded in the distance. I walked slowly to my door, opened it, and trudged into the kitchen.

I switched on the light, exposing the damage. The cabinet handle was bent. I leaned down to examine it and noticed that the entire handle had been twisted around and embedded into the wood. I pulled my sweat pants down and looked at my thigh. The bruise on my thigh was still bright red and a deep purple began to appear in the center. "Ouch," I said to myself.

I walked into the bathroom and stared in the mirror. My face was swollen. A fat lip, and remnants of black mascara running down my cheeks finished the beaten down look. "I wish I was dead" I thought.

The house is silent, and the aftermath of violence lingered in the air.

CHAPTER 53

*I*t was March 1977, and I finally made it to my 21st birthday. Disco clubs were popping up all over the Bay Area. Arthur and I took one day at a time, and I continued to hang on to a man who lusted after other women, who snorted cocaine daily, and who consumed gallons of alcohol. Arthur could barely keep his job, as a sheet metal fabricator, and I continued to enable him by pretending everything was fine.

On a typical Saturday evening, I sat in front of the T.V. watching "Who Knows What," alone. I thought back on our wedding day, and our honeymoon. Arthur and I had flown to San Diego and stayed at the Marriott Hotel for one week. It was a beautiful hotel with a lovely swimming pool. We took day trips in our rental car to the beach, restaurants, Sea World, and Balboa Zoo.

Balboa Zoo was just what I expected. There were animals living in a *friendly environment*. Most animals ignored most of the tourist. The on-lookers hollered and clapped their hands, hoping to get their attention. Arthur and I walked from display to display and stopped in front of the monkey *exploitation*. I watched Arthur as he lit a cigarette. It was not long before a monkey approached us. This alfa male locked on to my blue eyes and masturbated. I will never forget that look on

Arthur's face, the cigarette hanging from his mouth. He repeated over and over, "What the fuck?" The monkey finished within seconds, and I immediately turned away. I could hear Arthur laughing out loud, stooped over, stomping out his cigarette. "I hate zoos, let's get out of here Arthur," I requested we leave.

Oh, how I wished these animals were freed. Little boxes, little boxes. Zoos resembled little boxes. As we exited the zoo, I gazed at the American Flag; representing Freedom.

The sun began to set, and as evening slowly cast its shadow upon my empty living room, I jumped in surprise to the sound of our doorbell ringing. I rose to open the door, and I was delighted to see my friend, Susan. Susan was the second runner-up at our local beauty pageant. Susan and I had become close, as our husbands ran in the same *man club*, leaving their wives at home. Susan was tired of being left home alone too. "Let's go out Tess, don't sit here alone. There is a disco club in Castro Valley called the Piccadilly Pub. Let's go check it out!"

Deciding that it wasn't a bad idea, I changed into dancing attire, and put on some dancing shoes. Susan and I headed out the door and jumped into my car. "Let's go by Arthur's friend's house, Steve Jacobs. I want to see if Arthur is over there," I said. We drove up to Steve's house and sure enough, Arthur's truck was parked right in front.

I parked behind Arthur's truck and asked Susan to wait in the car. I walked up to the front door and rang the door-bell. Steve opened the door wide enough that I saw Arthur sitting on the couch with another woman. It appeared I had interrupted a foursome. I asked for Arthur to come outside. We argued on the lawn, and I became the angry, jealous, crazy wife. With a sudden burst of courage, I slapped him across the face.

I walked away and jumped into my car. Susan and I drove away. I drove to the disco club, ranting and raving all the way about what an idiot I was. Susan continues telling me to leave him, and I, the young naive girl, stupid in love, struggled with the idea of a failed marriage. "Shouldn't I be working on making the marriage work?"

"What marriage?" Susan asked me.

She was right. When would I find the courage to end it?

We arrived at the pub, and I freshened up my hair and makeup in the car. "Let's go dancing!" I said with enthusiasm. We entered the club and found a small table to sit at. The walls vibrated from the bass guitar and beat of the music. The music drove its way into my soul, and it wasn't long before I was on the dance floor with a nice man.

He leaned over and asked me, "Are you married, you are wearing a ring?"

"Yes, I am," I replied.

"Then why are you here?" he asked.

"I'm here to have some fun with my girlfriend. Is that a problem?"

He walked off the dance floor. Dejected, I slowly walked back to my table, looking down at the floor and thought about his question. *Why was I here?* The words resonated in my mind.

I suddenly felt hands on my shoulders from behind me. The tender hands turned me around. My eyes made their way up from the cowboy boots to the most beautiful brown eyes, with one small mole beneath each. I was held in a trance. "Let's dance, Tess Hamilton," Elio said with a smile. He took me by the hand and led me to the dance floor. The music changed to a slow song. Al Green serenaded, "How Can You Mend a Broken Heart." It was perfect.

Elio took my right hand and gently placed it around his waist. He took my left hand and held it tight in his. He moved me forward and back to the rhythm of the music. Turning, I followed his footsteps as he carried me lightly across the dance floor. We slowly circled around, bending our knees, gradually making our way up. My eyes were fixed on his when our lips met. Elio laid me back over his arm, suspending me in a melodic state. I trusted his touch as I relaxed into the safety of his arms. It seemed we were one. My dance partner glided over my miserable life.

I was dancing with Elio Lencioni, and for a gleaming moment, I felt elevated. I took in the scent of his endorphins, and I sunk within his arms. I took a deep breath, allowing my chest to rise against his. I recalled his bath, his skin, his chest as it rose up and down. I wanted that again, and my desire became insurmountable.

"Let's get out of here, Tess," Elio said as the music ended. I looked over at my friend Susan and motioned for her to come over. "I am with my old friend, George," Elio said. "You and your friend should come over to my house." I was energized, and thrilled with the prospect of spending time with Elio. I almost danced with Susan toward the exit.

Just then, Arthur made a grand entrance, with a woman on each arm. Instantly, my mind shifted, and I felt my blood boil. I became the jealous, angry wife again. I bolted forward, yelling at Arthur. His two escorts slithered by and disappeared into the club. The loud music drowned out my words. Our exchange of profanity continued out the entrance doors, ending under the moon's shadow. I noticed Susan making her way to my car, so I left to meet her.

I opened the car door and glanced at Elio watching me from across the street. I flushed with embarrassment and shame. He had never seen me like that. I fell into my car uncontrolled, unrestrained and completely frazzled. "What am I doing?" I ask Susan.

"Let's go over to Elio's house, you need to be around people who love you Tess," she said, "You cannot go home."

I maneuvered my way to Elio's house and pulled into the driveway. I missed this man. We walked up to the front door, glancing at the glowing porch light, and rang the doorbell. As the door opened, Elio's smile met my eyes. "You ok Tess?" he asked as he gently took my hand, "You were unhinged over there, was that your husband?"

"Yes, I am embarrassed to say, can we talk about anything other than him?" I asked.

"Yes, we can," Elio winked, and the four of us sat down at his kitchen table. Elio opened a bottle of wine, gently pouring the red liquid into four wine glasses.

George broke out a rock of cocaine and chopped up lines on a mirror. Susan and George snorted the white powder and handed the mirror to me. I thought about Arthur, the women he entertained, the abuse I endured, and the past year. I stared at the white snow.

I recalled the New Year's Eve when Lexie brought over some cocaine. It was shortly after Elio dumped me for the older woman.

She convinced me to try it, and we spent the evening with an ear to ear grin on our faces. We smoked a lot of cigarettes that night, and the drug seemed to enhance our perspective about all subjects imaginable.

"Tess, you don't have to do this," Elio snapped me back to the present. I looked at him and grabbed the mirror. I snorted the white marvel drug of the 70s and smiled. *Let's see what tonight will bring,* I told myself.

Susan, George, Elio and I spent the entire night talking, laughing, and analyzing every subject known to mankind. We sat at the kitchen table until the sun rose. I realized I was out all night, and I probably should go home. Arthur behaved this way, not me. Was this the new me? Who was I? I continued to ask myself; would I continue to be like this, or not? Round and round my mind went.

I admired Elio when he laughed and spoke. I tracked the lines on his forehead, and the wrinkles around his eyes. I noticed the whiteness of his teeth, and the wisp of hair that fell onto his ears. For the first time, I visualized with clarity, and I wondered, *will he ever say the words?*

I stood and approached Elio and reached for his hand. I heard music playing in the living room. The soft voice of Anne Murray singing "You Needed Me" whispered. I led him into the room and began a slow dance. He was not ordinary in any way. I drank in the aroma of his shirt, and I nestled my head against his warm chest.

Elio picked me up and carried me into his bedroom. Setting me onto his bed, no words were spoken as he undressed me. I closed my eyes and listened. Light showers seemed to dance on the quiet streets of morning, while I lavished his gentle touch.

CHAPTER 54

$\mathcal{N}$ight had fallen in San Francisco. I stood once I heard the honking of a car horn. My coworkers waited patiently outside. I was thrilled with the prospect of attending my first musical production, *Annie*. Arthur was out with his brother, again, and I was free from my misery for a night. I bounced out of my little box into an evening of enchantment.

I sat in the back seat, and Morgan drove us away. We traveled through the Oakland Cypress Street Viaduct. The concrete above and below seemed to feel as though we were traveling through *Bernoulli's* principle. The viaduct always gave me the creeps, and I quickly opened my window for air. I felt out of balance. However, once we made our way over to the Bay bridge, I felt relieved. We finally arrived in San Francisco at our first stop, Benihana's, for dinner.

The restaurant was a four-story venue. I was intrigued with the chefs in their uniforms, the chopping sounds, the smell of Japanese food cooking on hibachis. We were seated as a group of six on the fourth level. Juan ordered a round of Sakê, and set a small cup in front of me. "Leave him, Tess," he whispered. "I can make you happy."

I blushed and looked away, taking my first drink of Sakê. I pretended to not hear him. We ordered from the menu, and a chef appeared to cook and entertain us from his very hot grill. He began by juggling the salt and pepper shakers, moving on to juggle his knives. He chopped our steak, chicken, shrimp, and lobster all the while our rice and vegetables sizzled on the hibachi.

I chatted with coworkers while the aromas tugged on thoughts of Elio. He was the man who introduced me to life, love, and companionship. I bowed my head and inhaled the visions. I thought of his touch and the sound of his voice. I longed to put my arms around his waist as he cooked from his stove. From somewhere, the classical music by Paul Mauriat played the tune, "Love is Blue." Andre hovered in the background. The music was soft and faint.

The melody was immediately replaced by voices, and I sat with my friends. Juan smirked at me. His eyes drifted up and down my body. The chef played with our food, reminding me of the game Tiddlywinks, I played as a child. Our food flew onto our plates and landed perfectly still. The flavors melted in my mouth, cooked to perfection. The Sakē calmed my body. Life was good, or so it seemed, at that very moment. Juan rested his hand on my knee. I found it comforting in some strange and peculiar way. *"Was I desperate,"* I asked myself, *desperate for attention and affection?*

After we were all quite satisfied, we walked to the theatre around the corner. The bright lights of the theatre marquee lit up "Annie." We entered the double doors and made our way to our seats just behind the orchestra section. The lights dimmed.

The curtain opened to the stage set with rows of twin beds, and a cast of children sleeping in an orphanage. The children began singing as they rose from their beds, causing my heart to pound. Annie, a little red-headed girl, began singing with the most amazing voice. Her words flew out of her mouth and into my heart. This little girl took me into a world far away from the one I lived in. She became my center, my focus. She held my undivided attention for the remainder of the performance. She had no idea how she had captured my inner being. Tears flowed freely down my cheeks, as my ears listened to the notes they had never heard before.

When the production came to an end, my coworkers and I stood for the ovation. My smile went from ear to ear. "I love it!" I shouted as we continued to applaud. I hugged my program as we exited the theatre. The San Francisco air kissed my face, reminding me that I was part of the city, the lights, the sounds of distant ships, the hustle and bustle of people walking about, horns honking and laughter; oh, how I missed laughter.

I sang all the way home, "The sun will come out tomorrow." I felt loved, and I was uplifted until my friends and I arrived at my duplex.

I watched the car leave until I only heard silence. Standing on the curb, I looked up at the stars. The moon was full, and beams of light streamed down upon me. I turned and admired my ardent Karmann Ghia sitting in the driveway. I ran my hand across the smooth surface of the car.

The house was dark. No one was home. No one ever was.

CHAPTER 55

"Come on Tess, that should be an easy shot!" Lexie smiled as I struck my Viking pool cue, and sunk number 5 into the left corner pocket. Lexie was living with her high school sweetheart, John. The four of us gathered at the local pub for a game of pool. Lexie stood up straight, pondering her next shot. She was tall, slender, and had long wavy blonde hair. She and I competed in the beauty pageant and for the life of me, I could not figure out why she did not win. I was short and not even close to being as striking as she. I loved the memory of her piercing blue eyes captivating my drooling brother, Albert. Her Italian boyfriend, John, was very handsome, although he stood just a few inches below Lexie. Arthur and John got along well, and so we became a pleasant party of four.

We spent our time partying at their house in Hayward, and occasionally at my parents' cabin in the Sierra Nevada mountains. John graduated from being a user to becoming a dealer. Lexie was unaware of John's new job description; however, Arthur kept me informed, and I shared none of this with her. I wanted to shelter her from pain because I knew, all too well, what pain does when you love someone. I refused to be the channel of such pain in her life.

It was a very early morning in January 1977, when there was an abrupt knock on the entry door of John and Lexie's home. Lexie was fast asleep, but awoke suddenly when the police stormed through their bedroom. Lexie was forced to stand against the wall, with her hands and feet spread apart, naked and humiliated. They were arrested. Lexie was given her robe and hand cuffed. They were booked in Santa Rita State Prison in Pleasanton, California.

John entered a plea bargain with the district attorney, and sweet Lexie was never charged with a crime due to her ignorance of John's illegal drug operation.

AS I REMINISCED ABOUT LEXIE, I SAT IN SILENCE WHILE ARTHUR'S brother, Nate, repeated his vows to his new wife, Marcella. The music playing in the church, "Sunrise, Sunset" from *Fiddler on the Roof,* reminded me of Andre. Andre reminded me of Brazil and that person I used to be. A part of me was happy that Nate finally settled down. This did not stop Arthur, however, he just hung out with other single friends. As we moved our way to the wedding reception hall, I glanced across the room and noticed a familiar face. The woman's eyes met mine, and I recalled Arthur's indiscretions.

One-night Arthur laid asleep by my side. I was quiet, listening to his breathing. He mumbled, and I decided to humor myself and ask him questions. "Who are you speaking to, Arthur?"

"Why, you of course, Rene."

"Rene who?" I asked.

"Blubber," his voice sounded agitated. I began to shake Arthur, waking him from his pleasant dream state.

"Who is Rene Blubber?" I asked. He just stared at me, his green eyes remained foggy, and rolled over ignoring my questions. "No one makes up names in your sleep, no one" I mumbled as I left his bedside, and headed into the bathroom. I could not hold back the tears.

I removed my prescription bottle from the medicine cabinet, and counted each pill, one by one, and stopped at 25. I looked up at myself again and stood staring at my reflection. I hated Arthur, and I hated his friends. I had channeled all my resentment towards Steve, and somehow deep in my heart, I knew that was wrong.

~

STEVE JACOBS, WHO HAD BECOME ANOTHER ONE OF ARTHUR'S COCAINE connections. Steve, single of course, was dating a girl one year older than me named Celine. She was nice, but we really had nothing in common. However, I yearned to feel accepted by Arthur's friends, that way I could mingle in their circle with Arthur by my side. I needed to change my strategy. "Keep your friends close, but keep your enemies closer."

It had become my new typical Saturday night, spending the evening at Steve's house. Celine and I sat chatting away about this, that, and whatever. I glanced over at Steve and Arthur as they snorted lines of white powder and inhaled a nicotine chaser. Celine mentioned she was looking for a new roommate; her current one was moving out. We bounced around names of people. I casually asked if I knew her roommate? Celine said no, however, I pressed again and asked, "What is her name?" and she replied, "Rene Blubber."

~

I PRESSED MY HANDS AGAINST MY FOREHEAD AND GAZED AT THE bathroom floor. I stood in silence as countless nights flooded into my mind. Nights alone, staring at the television. Nights when Arthur returned in the wee hours of the morning. Nights following baseball games. Baseball games that included Steve, and Celine, and Rene? The night I surprised Arthur at Steve's party of four, and the same night Arthur entered the Piccadilly Pub with a woman on each arm.

"Tess, I do not know what is going on between Arthur and Rene, but leave me out of it," Celine insisted. My brain swirled with confusion, as I recalled her passing a mirror to me with lines of cocaine on it. I waved my hand and shook my head no. I was done. I walked out the front door, and made my way down the empty streets of San Leandro, to my dark duplex.

I thought of Lexie's naked body up against the wall. I remembered her broken heart, and I longed to speak to her. John's entire family returned to Pennsylvania (part of the plea bargain). She and John followed, both leaving the life of drugs behind. They gave their relationship a clean start, and a new beginning.

"A new beginning," I whispered.

I was broken, and my heart waved the white flag. I heard the faint sound of voices hollering, "Tess, come back, Tess, Tess."

I rummaged through past nights. A night when I came home unexpectedly, and found Arthur with a woman casually drinking wine, as they relaxed on our couch. I went crazy that night and told her to leave. Arthur escorted her outside to her car. And that is when I really lost it. I walked out into the dark night and stood between *her* and my husband. Arthur was drunk and after she drove away, I slammed him to the ground and pounded on his chest, ripping his shirt off. He outweighed me, but the adrenaline kicked in. I had become a bionic bitch. My fingertips twitched at the thought.

I could still hear the music at Nate and Marcella's wedding reception. I tried very hard to visualize that woman across the room, staring back at me. Was that Rene Blubber, who had sat on our couch and entered the Pub?

Too many struggles had passed since my wedding day. Thoughts of leaving flew through my head. I no longer wanted to leave Arthur, I wanted to leave my existence.

I shook the bottle of pills and contemplated.

CHAPTER 56

*A*s I shifted my way in and out of the San Francisco Bay Area, I turned up the volume to hear Stevie Wonder's, "I Wish." It took me back to 1977.

~

THE WHITE PHONE MOUNTED ON THE KITCHEN WALL RANG. I PICKED UP the receiver to hear Lexie's voice on the other end. Lexie was angry. Her voice cracked, and she struggled to find her words. She was leaving John and moving back to California. "I can't take the pressure of his family and John fell into some abusive habits." I was familiar with those.

What is it with men growing up in this community? Has domestic violence become ingrained in their character?

Lexie's biological father worked in the film industry in sunny Hollywood. He had invited her to live on his yacht in the beautiful harbor that surrounded Marina del Rey. Lexie accepted his offer and shared her travel plans with me. Hope and prospective opportunity filled up her voice.

"Come visit me there," she said, and it was not long before I took her offer seriously. I called the toll-free phone number for Pacific Southwest Airlines or PSA.

I waited in anticipation as the PSA operator answered. With the help of my new Visa credit card, I booked a round trip flight from Oakland to Los Angeles, California. My flight departed on May 24th.

It was warm and busy when I entered the Los Angeles terminal. The ocean air was pleasant and took on a different smell than the San Francisco Bay. I waited in anticipation of seeing my dear friend Lexie. She had taken a waitressing job for a well-known venue near the courthouse. Many celebrities frequented the spot, and she became acquainted with influential people in Hollywood.

Lexie moved from the marina and into an apartment in Santa Monica. She had gained two roommates and quickly settled into the fast lane of Southern California. I noticed a tall, blonde, and Hollywood beautiful woman standing near the luggage carousel. She motioned to me and as I approached; she introduced herself as Mary, Lexie's roommate.

Mary and I drove to Lexie's employer, Cheerios Restaurant. I was thrilled to see Lexie as we arrived in the lobby area. Lexie seated me at a small table, and Mary exited shortly afterwards.

I observed Lexie as she maneuvered in and out of packed tables, working steadily until her shift ended. I admired the way she interacted with customers. I couldn't help but notice the high-end vehicles that lined the street, just outside a window to my left.

As the day neared its end, Lexie, and I drove to her apartment. "Guess what we are doing tomorrow, Tess?" Lexie grinned. "We are attending the opening night for Star Wars, the movie!"

Star Wars was the most expected upcoming feature since I can't remember when. That we were attending was exhilarating. Both of us found it hard to fall asleep that night.

The big marquee with the title, "Star Wars," came into view as Lexie and I approached Westwood Theatre at Mann Village. We traveled in her silver 1966 Mustang and parked in the parking lot around the corner. We took our place in a long line that looped around the side street and settled into our four-hour wait.

We finally entered the packed theatre, sitting right in the middle on the upper level for the sold-out production. The lights dimmed, and music began. The crowd hollered in expectation, and I was immediately drawn into the story, the characters, and the plot. It captured everyone in attendance, and during the two-hour creation, people cheered and clapped.

At the end of the movie, the entire audience stood for a standing ovation. It was a smash hit. I felt so lucky to be a part of it. The movie was beyond any expectation I had, and it exceeded all imaginable dreams. Lexie and I stopped at a local pub on our way home. The movie seemed to be the hot topic around town.

The next morning, Lexie dropped me off at a set of condominiums in Marina del Rey. She had many new friends that lived there, and I would be well taken care of while she worked. It was a beautiful hot sunny day, and I brought my bright orange Brazilian "tanga" swimsuit to wear. I was greeted by Mary at the door. She, evidently, stayed here frequently with her boyfriend. Mary showed me to his room, to change, and invited me to join them on their private beach area.

The sandy beach had rows of volleyball nets, and long phone cords attached to princess-line phones. Everyone seemed to be grossly engaged in some form of conversation on their phones. I confidently came out in my swimsuit, and I watched Lexie's friends slowly raised their sun glasses. I was fair skinned and the sun in Marina del Rey was intense. They warned me not to stay outside too long. However, I had lived in Brazil and entertained the beaches of Copacabana, Ipanema, Aparecida, and I felt I was quite capable of timing my sun exposure.

As I basked in the warm sun, I thought about my life at home. My life with Arthur. I felt sick. I envied Lexie and wished so much I was single. What was I thinking when I said yes to him? I tried to focus on the days ahead. I heard a faint voice, then the touch of Mary's hand. "Tess, you should roll over," she whispered. I turned onto my backside and squinted through my Vuarnete sunglasses at the light stratus layer above. I noticed an airliner passing in and out of the clouds at 30 thousand feet. I wondered who was up there?

My fair skin turned a light shade of red, and Lexie's friends became concerned. "Tess, you should go into the condo, and get out of the sun." I pushed my forefinger against my thigh, and it left a white mark. It appeared I had stayed out too long.

I remained inside, that is, until a handsome young man arrived. He introduced himself as Tom; another good friend of Lexie. Tom invited me to take in the scenery along the Malibu coastline. He owned a beautiful Lamborghini convertible, and I quickly accepted his offer. We drove the coastal area, and Tom pointed out the beautiful houses that lined the hills. There were crowds of people at the public beaches, and many stop lights.

Tom undressed me with his eyes, making it obvious when he lifted his sunglasses to gawk. He thought I was pretty enough to be a model, or a movie star, or better yet... a beauty pageant queen! This amused me, and I recalled the fortune teller in Bahia, Brazil. She said I would become famous one day.

Tom pulled up in front of Cheerios restaurant, and we waited for Lexie to end her shift. He leaned over to kiss me, and I turned away. "I am married," I protested.

Tom sweetly said, "So am I."

He reminded me of Noel in Brazil. My body resisted, and the words "Don't touch me" probed at me. I was appalled. Time moved at a snail's pace as we waited for Lexie.

Lexie bounced out of Cheerios, and I said goodbye to Mr. Lamborghini. He drove away, seemingly frustrated.

That evening, as Lexie and I met more of her friends at the Wharf for dinner, she decided to introduce me to escargot with garlic and parsley butter. It appeared that she had acquired a taste for the finer things in life, and I was delighted to try them. I savored the flavor, and swallowed the chewy, garlic flavored snail. We enjoyed our main course that included filet mignon and lobster. It reminded me of Elio, and I brushed the thought quickly away.

As we ended our evening with a drive to her Santa Monica one-bedroom apartment, my sunburn began to hurt. I was overwhelmed with nausea, and shortly upon entering Lexie's place, I puked up a delicious cuisine. I tried to lay down and quickly realized I could not.

The back of my legs, my buttocks, and my entire back were burned. My skin had tightened up and the effort to walk became difficult. The night was full of endless pain, and I wished for the soothing conversation from a bus driver in Bahia. I imagined my flight home would be equally uncomfortable. Lexie applied baking soda to my skin, and I struggled to fall asleep.

~

It wasn't long before I gazed out of the window of my PSA Boeing 727 flight inbound to Oakland, California.

My short vacation ended, with the voice of Stevie Wonder playing over the radio, in my Karmann Ghia. Thoughts flooded my mind as I drove down the boulevard closer to home. Oakland Airport, along with LAX, faded in the distance, and the arrival at my dark home drew near.

I looked straight ahead out of the windshield, but all I could see was *a galaxy far-far away.*

CHAPTER 57

ecember 1978 brought with it a familiar chill. On Christmas morning, Arthur and I began our day, opening a gift exchanged between the two of us. Arthur purchased a set of golf clubs for me and seemed eager to get me started playing golf. I purchased a suede bomber style jacket and a wool scarf for Arthur. He seemed pensive as we settled into a *happy* married life again. The fights between us seemed like distant memories, and I was once again optimistic.

Arthur's family welcomed me into their home for a wonderful Christmas Day Dinner. Arthur's mother and father were gracious people, and he had two beautiful sisters. Arthur's oldest brother was enlisted in the U.S. Army and lived abroad. His three remaining siblings, along with Nate's wife Marcella, joined us as we enjoyed a beautiful dinner.

It was obvious to me how much Arthur's mother loved him. She doted over him continually, and at times I felt he took full advantage of her good nature. Arthur was coddled growing up; it explained his narcissistic behavior. Things appeared good on the surface, but I was guarded around Arthur, and even more insecure than ever. I often thought of Elio and then tried very hard to love my husband. I jumped easily, and at times I flinched when Arthur gestured while talking. His older sister noticed and raised one eyebrow at me from across the table. I looked down at my hands, folded neatly on my lap.

The evening drew to a close when Arthur and I said our goodbyes and traveled home. It was a rainy Christmas evening, and I watched the wiper blades travel back and forth across the windshield. I thought of the wipers on the station wagon my Colombian father drove through the streets of Bogota. The street lights were lined with garland and Christmas twinkle.

I continued looking at the road ahead of us. When Arthur opened his Christmas package this morning, he seemed pleased with his jacket. As I had sat watching him, along-side our small Christmas tree, my eyes drifted. His jacket seemed to turn into a leather coat, longer and much more expensive. I flashed back the day Elio and I Christmas shopped. I could smell the leather and see the brown eyes gleaming, and my heart raced. I shook it off as we turned the corner and down our street.

I noticed the mailbox on the corner, and then I remembered my mother. It was night, and she was walking home from the bus stop. She walked at a fast pace, and I ran to catch up with her at that very mailbox. I was barely a teenager, and I could not contain my excitement to see her. She was cold, and I smiled when we met. I recalled countless letters I dropped in that mailbox, letters to Andre.

I lowered my head as Arthur and I pulled into our driveway. The same driveway I grew up playing jump rope on when my brother died. The same ticky-tacky house I spent growing up in, where my father fashioned airplanes and sailboats. It was the same house my father remodeled into a duplex. It was my home, and now Arthur and I lived here. What used to be my sanctuary became my *darkness*.

We weren't home long, before I heard the familiar words, "I am going out Tess, I will be home later." I did not argue anymore. I only heard the door close, and the sound of his truck pulling away from the front curb. I brushed my teeth, washed my face, and retired. I laid in bed, and wondered what life would be like, if I was to live alone? I imagined being on a date, and smiling, maybe even dancing with someone. It was a welcoming thought that lulled me to sleep.

The sound of pots and pans clanking in the kitchen, along with a loud Yesterday & Today wailing from the stereo, woke me from my deep sleep. Arthur was home and decided he was hungry. I looked at the clock alongside our bed, and it was 3:00 a.m.

I groggily rose out of bed and walked into the kitchen. Arthur stood over the stove cooking potatoes and eggs. "What are you doing?" I asked.

"I am cooking, are you blind?" he replied.

"I have to work in the morning, can you lower the volume on the stereo?" I hollered. Arthur continued cooking and ignored me. I smelled the booze on his breath from across the kitchen. I walked over to the stereo and lowered the volume. I returned to the bedroom and closed our wood louver doors. I climbed into our bed and tried to return to sleep. Within minutes, the volume rose, and I was once again listening to bass pounding, drum smashing, electrical guitar music.

I was getting angry, and this time I bolted out of bed and into the living room. I turned the music down and returned to bed. No sooner that my head hit the pillow, the volume went back up, and this time it was louder.

I got up a third time and stood at the kitchen door. "Please Arthur, turn it down!" I pled with him. He continued to ignore me, and I returned to the bedroom to bury my head in my pillow. Within seconds, I heard Arthur's fist go through the louver doors, and wood flew everywhere. The wood seemed to travel in slow motion, landing on the floor. I sprang up in bed, to see Arthur displaying his full fury. His green eyes blazed, his nostrils flared, and he snorted just like the beautiful horses that pounded back and forth across the polo field in Brazil. Arthur was not beautiful when he was angry.

I stood as he approached one side of our water bed. I ran the opposite direction, across the top of our bed, side stepping pieces of wood, and towards the back door. Arthur raced to catch me, reaching out and grabbing my hair. I tumbled to the ground, and he pounded my head up and down against the floor.

I didn't freeze. I fought back and managed to get away from his grip. I was not wearing the buster brown saddle shoes, but I figured if I could kick free from four young men, then how can one hold me down? I sprinted out the door and into our driveway. I ran into memories that flashed before me. I saw neighborhood kids playing *kick-the-can,* and I became the giant Andy Warhol poster. My bare feet carried me up the concrete steps to safety, and now, years later, I could see that I was not waddling.

I frantically hollered, "Help, let me in, help!" I realized I was half naked, standing in my small silk camisole top with matching hot pants. I kept looking over my shoulder and continued pounding, and finally, the door opened.

I ran into the arms of Angie's husband, Mel. He quickly closed the door and grabbed a blanket to cover me. "What is happening Tess?" he asked. I was shaking, crying, and I couldn't speak. My sister Angie got up and comforted me.

"What is wrong with me, why me?" I finally said, "Why me?"

Angie tried to comfort me, but I was too consumed by my own thoughts.

We heard Arthur start his truck and peel out down the street. "I am leaving him," I said. "I don't know where I will go, but I am leaving."

I walked back to my home, and looked at the broken door, the food on the stove, and then I noticed my purse had been dumped out; the contents splayed across the floor. My money was gone from my wallet, and my car keys were missing.

I laid in bed and waited as the sun found its way over the coastal fog. I dressed for work, packed a suitcase, and headed out to my car. Within seconds, I remembered that my keys were taken. I returned to the kitchen and phoned Arthur's mother, asking her to come over. "I need a ride to work," I explained. It felt good, knowing that she would see the damage in the house, and perhaps she would realize how messed up her son truly was.

I sat and waited for her to arrive. My hands shook with nervousness. I walked into the bathroom and looked at myself again. I was an abused wife, and I no longer liked myself. I felt worthless. The doorbell interrupted my berating.

I opened the door, and Mrs. Mother-In-Law entered my home. "What has happened, Tess?" she asked.

"Look around," I said, "This is what your son has done. It's a good thing I got away, or I would be broken apart, just like our louvre doors."

My dear sweet Mother-in-law looked around and then looked at me. "Oh, I am so sorry Tess, whatever you do.... just.... don't be too hard on him."

My mouth dropped open, and my mind went blank. I couldn't find the words, and I couldn't understand the logic in her statement. I looked at her in amazement and wondered. Was domestic violence somehow acceptable in her world? "Hard on him.... No one has been hard enough on him!" I shouted. She glared at me, as though I was the cause of the fiasco.

We both walked out of the house and to her car. She looked over at mine, and asked, "Why do you need a ride to work, Tess, when your car is parked right here?"

"Because Arthur took my car keys," I dryly responded.

"Any idea where he might be?" she asked.

"No, he just left," I said.

We drove to the great white hospital on the hill in Hayward. I thanked Mrs. Mother-in-law and made my way to the X-ray department.

I watched my feet, as I put one foot in front of the other, and counted each step. One, two, three, *four*. "*Four*," I said to myself. *Fore*. I see the golf balls pass by at Willow Park Country Club, as Arthur and I say our vows. I heard the voices of Loggins and Messina, singing "The Love Song." I see my sister Angie, holding her newborn baby Paul, smiling at me, as Arthur and I turned around to greet our guests, as man and wife. I see our guests clapping, and the band setting up for our reception. I see my white shoes under my white wedding gown, remembering the penny my father dropped in my shoe for good luck.

I see my beautiful white satin shoes fade into white leather nursing shoes.

Five, six, seven, eight. I entered the building and punched my time card. I observed the rows of time cards as I placed mine back in my slot. I placed it perfectly straight, and in line with the others. I remembered uniform rows of Walnut Orchards, and then I began working another day.

CHAPTER 58

*I*t was a bitter cold morning, but the sun was shining when I loaded my Karmann Ghia with everything I could fit into it. I made sure I had my golf clubs, snow skis, ski boots, sleeping bag, pillow, favorite albums, and clothes. I made a stop at the local automotive parts store and picked up a set of snow chains for my tires. As I pulled out of the parking lot, I turned on the radio and entered the freeway heading east. I watched the mountains ahead and listened to the easy-going melody played by Billy Joel. I turned up the volume while "Leave me Alone" played. I sang along and smiled to the words. They seemed to narrate my moment perfectly. I thought back over the past two years, staring out into my new frontier horizon, and wondered what was next? I noticed a large semi-truck ahead, and I moved up alongside it. The driver looked down at me, and I was grinning from ear to ear.

~

"I love you, don't leave me," Arthur said while tears were flowing down his face. He tore at my heartstrings, pulling them one at a time. "I cannot stay any longer," I repeated, while pacing back and forth across our living room carpet. "If you love me, truly love me Arthur, then let me go!"

~

I RECENTLY HAD ACCEPTED A POSITION IN THE OFFICE OF DR. DOLT, A gastroenterologist, and internal medicine physician. Dr. Dolt was a good doctor, but he was also a cheater, with many mistresses. Dr. Dolt hid, nothing. Each morning, he purchased a bouquet of daisies for his mistress at the local hospital. She worked in the business office. He made his early morning rounds there, before arriving at our office. Dr. Dolt boasted about his behavior and discussed his relationship with her. He bragged about setting up house in a small apartment in San Leandro, just for the two of them. He had a college trust fund for her two children. He reminded me of Dr. Zhivago and Lara.

Dr. Dolt had a beautiful wife named Emily. They adopted a girl named Sarah, and a boy named Samuel. Emily stopped by our office occasionally, and I tried to remain upbeat when visiting with her.

Once a year, Dr. Dolt took his wife to Sun Valley, Idaho for a ski trip. She looked forward to their time away from each year. This year, Dr. Dolt asked if I would stay in their home for the week, and take care of their children. He offered to pay my regular salary while working in his home.

I accepted and jumped at the opportunity to be away from Arthur. It would be a vacation for me as well.

Samuel and Sarah were a joy to watch. Samuel was four, and Sarah was five. They were very smart and lived in a beautiful home that overlooked the San Francisco Bay. I protected the children from Arthur and explained to him that he was not allowed to stay over with me. I did not trust his behavior around the children.

When I arrived for my temporary job, I parked my Karmann Ghia in their four-car garage. I was allowed to drive their 1978 Mercedes Benz. It was a big luxury car that I enjoyed transporting the kids around town in. I relished in the lifestyle and imagined myself happily married with children.

I phoned Arthur in the evenings, after the children were in bed, to see how he was doing. The phone rang and rang, but Arthur never seemed to be home. "He is probably enjoying my absence," I reminded myself. I contemplated ways to leave him, as I sunk into the king-size bed. I nestled into silk sheets and smothered myself in a big goose feathered blanket.

"Go home, Tess," Arthur's big sister's mouth spewed. The words rang in my head as I wandered in and out of sleep. I tossed and turned, waking in a sweat.

I lumbered about this big beautiful house and stopped to admire the grand piano. I remembered Dr. Dolt playing a piece from *Fiddler on the Roof*. He was so talented, rich and lucky. "Lucky," I said to myself. Lucky to be successful. Lucky to have a devout wife and family. Lucky to have a beautiful home. Lucky to be a doctor. And then I remembered his other women.

Unlucky, is Emily? Unlucky, am I? Emily and I lived in two distinct and opposite worlds, and yet the men we married seek the love of other women. I was perplexed, as I continued my walk around the palatial home.

I stopped and gazed out of the picture windows. I leaned down and opened the sliding glass doors over-looking the San Francisco Bay. I looked to my left, and saw the skyline of the San Mateo Bridge, glowing in the distance.

I looked to my right, to see the lights that lined each cable on the Bay Bridge, as it twinkled between the hovering fog. I visualized a black Porsche driving over and into the city. I saw his eyes smiling at me, and then I looked beyond my memories to expose the city.

I REMINISCED ABOUT THE NIGHTS THAT ARTHUR DID NOT RETURN FROM his softball games. Arthur was on a men's softball team, and they played every Friday night. After I worked all day, Arthur was usually gone by the time I arrived at home. I would have a light dinner, and wait for him. Sometimes, it would be early evening when he returned.

Other nights, he would phone, and I would meet him for pizza and beer at our local Porky's Pizza Palace. Then there were the nights that he would arrive home the next day, still in uniform. I would worry most of the night, pacing back and forth, and imagine the most awful things.

One particular wee hour of the morning, I decided to call the emergency rooms, police departments, and friends, hoping to find him. All my calls came up empty-handed, and so I found myself driving around the dark, deserted streets of San Leandro looking for him.

I arrived at a four-corner stop sign, and my husband's older sister pulled alongside me. She rolled down her window, "What are you doing Tess?" she inquired.

"I am looking for your brother, I am worried," I replied.

"Go home, Tess, go home!" she hollered. She rolled her eyes and drove off.

She had a look on her face that said, "You are a fool, Tess."

I made a U-turn and headed back to my home.

I LOOKED ABOUT DR. DOLT'S MAGNIFICENT HOME. I POSITIONED THE throw pillows on the couch in exact precision. I admired the photographs of Dr. Dolt and Emily on their wedding day. I raised one eyebrow and returned to bed.

Money does not prevent darkness; however, the thought of having just a bit more of it would be nice. After all, isn't that what Topol said in *Fiddler on the Roof*? As I stared at the walls of this beautiful master bedroom, I pretended they were mine, and I fell fast asleep.

CHAPTER 59

*A*s I continued driving East toward the Sierra Nevada Mountains, feelings of hatred flowed through my head. I thought about my final days with Dr. Dolt, and my final hours with Arthur.

~

DR. DOLT IGNITED ANOTHER AFFAIR WITH ONE OF THE REGISTERED nurses at the hospital. Her name was Diane. She was a pretty nurse, that frequently stopped by our office to see him.

Emily and the children took a trip back to Pennsylvania each year to visit her family. When they departed on their annual trip, Dr. Dolt talked openly about his RN interlude.

He explained how he transported her in the back seat of his Mercedes Benz, and covered her with a blanket, until they arrived safely in the garage of his home. Then, he closed the electric garage door with his remote control. They stayed in the house, slept in the same bed he shared with Emily, and in the morning, she left in the same manner that she arrived.

I was appalled, and scolded him, but he just laughed at me, and carried on as if he did no wrong.

One day, I told him, when the second coming of Christ occurs, he would be left behind. He laughed, and boasted about being Jewish, and not believing in Christ. I shook my head and continued discounting his words. I told myself it was just not right. He was married, and he carried on and didn't even try to hide it.

A year had passed, and I continued working for this Blowfish, full of himself, physician.

It happened on a Wednesday, and we did not see patients on Wednesday. I was ten minutes late. As I entered the office, Dr. Dolt was sitting at his desk in his private office, and I said, "Good morning."

"You are late," he said and motioned me into his office.

"I am sorry, it won't happen again," I said as I took a seat in front of his desk.

Dr. Dolt scowled at me and explained that my behavior was no longer acceptable. He reported that other physicians have complained about my phone manners. He told me that I was not the person he hired, and I should never work in this type of environment again. Dr. Dolt spoke in detail, that he was letting me go. However, he magnanimously offered, "You can stay until you find another job."

I sat listening to the words that flowed from his mouth, feeling paralyzed. I heard him, but I kept thinking about the bottom line. I was getting fired from my job. I sat in silence, as he continued to belittle me, and berate my character. I watched his big mouth, with his big lips open and close, his big eyebrows moved up and down, his big nostrils moved in and out, while his big hands waved about. He was so unattractive. I wondered how he had so many mistresses. "Must be the money," I told myself.

Dr. Dolt puffed himself up, stood, and walked around the desk in his big expensive suit, and his big expensive shoes. He tried to comfort me, but I pushed him away. "Don't touch me," I screamed in my head, but my lips never parted, and I returned to my desk. "You can go home Tess, take today off. I can see you are upset. Come back tomorrow, Tess. You still have a job," Dr. Dolt said, while looking down at me.

I left the office and drove back to my home. Arthur was still sleeping, because Arthur never worked.

I immediately picked up the phone and called my father. I waited while the phone rang once, twice, three times. I heard Father's voice say hello, and I cried. "I need to leave here, and I don't know what to do?" I begged. "I was fired, Father. My husband, well you know. I can't take anymore, please help me."

Father instructed me to compose a letter for Dr. Dolt. I took notes as he dictated to me. Father assured me that all would be fine. "Write the letter, and give it to the doctor tomorrow Tess, then I want you to load up your car, and drive here. I will put you to work, and you can work for your mother and me," he said.

I hung up the phone and wrote my letter.

I instructed Dr. Dolt to provide a great letter of recommendation. I notified him that I will work through Friday, and that will be my last day of work.

I recalled when Father and Mother moved away. They opened a business of their own and were living in our cabin in the mountains. Arthur and I rented one side of my childhood home, while my sister Angie and her husband, Mel, rented the front section. It seemed perfect, but as life played out, nothing was perfect.

I folded the letter and slipped it into an envelope. I walked over and looked at Arthur asleep in bed. I scanned the contents of our home and looked for only the important things I needed. I planned. I quietly took out items that wouldn't be missed, like my skis and golf clubs, and put them in my car. I washed the dishes and loaded clothes in the washing machine. Arthur heard me in the kitchen. "Tess? Why are you home?" he hollered from the bedroom.

I walked over to the room and stood in the doorway. "I was fired," I said, and walked back into the kitchen. Arthur quietly slipped his arms around my waist. He kissed my neck, and whispered in my ear, "I love you; we can work this out."

I stood frozen in front of the sink. I tried to find the words. Arthur spun me around, picked me up, and carried me off to bed.

I SHIFTED DOWN TO THIRD GEAR AND EXITED THE FREEWAY. I STOPPED for gas, and as I stood next to my car filling up my tank, I could smell the change. It was crisp and clean, with the fragrance of pine trees. I looked to the mountains, and they were closer. I no longer viewed the San Francisco Bay. The gas pump shut off, and I hung up the nozzle. I entered the gas station office and paid for my gas. The man behind the counter smiled, and I walked outside; glancing at the newspaper stand. The headline caught my attention. It was January 19, 1979, Attorney General John N. Mitchell was released on parole, and I pondered. I could relate. I felt as though I was just released from federal prison, except I was in California, and John N. Mitchell was in Alabama.

I jumped in my car, turned up the heat and continued heading east. I listened to the music of Lynyrd Skynyrd singing "Sweet Home Alabama," and my mind spun. Was that written about John Mitchell?

I was free; I was alive. I passed that truck earlier, and it seemed to portray faces of the past; faces that no longer held me back. They faded in the rear-view mirror.

Lexie was correct. She said I was holding on to a thread, and one day it would break, or I would *just let go*. I think it was both.

CHAPTER 60

"Get off of me!" I hollered as Arthur tried to make love to me. I was not in any condition, emotionally or otherwise. "I wrote a letter to Dr. Dolt," I explained, as I fell out of bed.

"Come on Tess, you have the day off, and we should take advantage of it!" Arthur grappled to get me.

"No, I am not in the mood Arthur," I said. Arthur is not one to accept rejection and grew angry. His eyes squinted, and his lip curled. I walked over to the stereo and selected The Cars. The song played, and I swayed back and forth, and listened to the lyrics of "Good Times Roll." Trying to ignore my husband, I danced with my *thoughts of leaving.*

I felt my husband pull me in close to his chest. His arms were strong, and the touch of his hands felt rough. The cigarette, and alcohol smell, lingered on his body, and repulsed me. He rocked back and forth with me, and I felt his erection against my body.

"Come on, Tess," he whispered. I felt as though I was trapped, and the only way out was to succumb. Arthur picked me up and carried me back to bed. He got everything he wanted.

I made love to Arthur with every ounce of anger reserved within me. I handled him as rough as he handled me. We threw each other against the bed, and the movement of the water beneath us rocked us back and forth. Arthur was totally aroused. "Why don't you make love like this all the time, Tess?" he whispered, as he licked my ear. I heard the song change to "You're All I've Got Tonight." He yanked on my long blonde hair and laughed as he bit my lower lip. I kissed him hard and dug my nails deep into his back. Arthur cried out and quickly flipped me over onto my stomach. He continued pulling on my hair, and I felt his deep penetration. As Arthur reached his moment of ecstasy, the narcissist did not even notice that I never reached mine.

It's a masquerade party, and I played out my part with a vengeance. We both dropped from exhaustion. Our hearts pounded, and sweat poured off our chests. I felt nothing but hatred for him. Arthur collapsed into a deep sleep, and as I laid beside my husband, I planned my escape. "Bye-Bye-Love" played in the background.

"How poetic," I smirked.

"WHAT DO YOU MEAN, TOMORROW IS YOUR LAST DAY?" DR. DOLT exclaimed.

"Yes, that is correct Dr. Dolt. You see, I am working through tomorrow, and I expect a letter of recommendation from you, and my final paycheck," I said.

"I am not writing a letter Tess, that is not happening," Dr. Dolt continued, "I will have your final paycheck ready for you, however the letter is out."

"Dr. Dolt," I continued, "If you do not write a letter of recommen-dation, then I have no choice but to file a complaint with the American Medical Association. I will state that you made numerous sexual advances towards me, and when I denied you of these advances, you fired me."

Dr. Dolt's big mouth dropped open, and his big brown eyes stared at mine. "You wouldn't," he said.

"Try me," I dueled him with my eyes.

The pendulum on Dr. Dolt's wall clock swung back and forth. I felt the electrical current of his rage transfer across the room and into my body. I looked at him for a response. "Who would believe you?" I asked, as I raised one eyebrow.

Dr. Dolt let out a deep breath and spilled the words that sweetly rang in my ears. "I will have that letter, and your paycheck tomorrow Tess."

~

I GLANCED DOWN AT THE SEAT NEXT TO ME AND PICKED UP THE envelope Dr. Dolt had given to me. I smiled with satisfaction. "Father will be so proud," I whispered. I turned up the radio, looked out the window at the mountains. They were covered in snow. "Snow," I said to myself.

~

BLOOD FLOWED FROM ARTHUR'S WRIST. "WHAT HAVE YOU DONE?" I asked, as Arthur appeared from the bathroom. "Don't leave me, Tess", he sobbed. Arthur slit both his wrists, and I stood helpless, bewildered, with feelings of guilt. This fish bowl of insanity consumed my every thought as I ran to the medicine cabinet for bandages.

It was my lunch hour, and I dashed home for a quick lunch, and to tell Arthur I was leaving him. I called Mrs. Mother in Law, because she was a registered nurse, and because we were dealing with her son. She promised to come over right away, and I reassured Arthur he would not die. Arthur's wrists appeared to be slightly cut, and the blood spewing from his wrists had slowed to a near stop. He was so dramatic, and he obviously stopped at nothing to prevent me from leaving. It was not long before his mother arrived, and I returned to work.

I was once again returning late, and I apologized to Dr. Dolt. He rolled his eyes and walked away as I began answering phone calls and scheduling appointments.

I said nothing about Arthur and kept my feelings inside. I found it hard to focus on work. Flashes burst through my mind of blood running down Arthur's hands, driving around countless nights looking for him, calling hospitals and police departments, and discovering Arthur with other women. I thought back to a night when Arthur locked himself in our bathroom, snorting his stash of white powder that he held so dear. I struggled to support us financially.

I must get out of here. I felt trapped. I was trapped, when Grandfather interrogated me in that motel room. I was trapped, when I slept in the home at Laguna Seca Ranch.

I was trapped, when my step-grandfather took my sister, and then later took me. I was trapped, as I sat in a locked room waiting to see my father. My mind was in a fog when Dr. Dolt came back into focus. He sickened me as well.

Friday came to an end, and as I left the office (envelope in hand), I said *nothing* with a smile. I thought about how Catholics do not eat meat on Fridays and I wondered, "What does this Jewish doctor eat on Fridays?"

"I hope its crow," I said, as I closed the door to his office of Alimentary Canals.

CHAPTER 61

$\mathcal{T}$he winding road of Highway 88 took me further and further into the mountains. The two-lane highway made its way around pine trees and canyons painted in yellows and reds. There were rushing streams of white and crystal blue. The light dusting of snow had fallen on each branch, and the sunlight floated between the branches, leaving a fine mist of moisture swirling up and into the horizon. The only sound was my engine winding down, with constant shift changes as I rounded each turn, and made the gradual climb further up in elevation. I no longer had radio reception, and I felt as though I had entered the *Colors of Twilight.*

Elio consumed my heart. I missed his soft touch, his kindness and respect. I tried to balance the reasons he rejected me. "Why he did not love me?" I asked myself repeatedly. My body felt like it would explode from heart ache. My chest was tight, and I tried to stay focused on the future. My fingers tingled while my shifting motions turned more and more abrupt. I had become anxious. I spotted a phone booth in the small town of Pine Grove. I pulled over and walked to the booth. I scrambled through my wallet and counted enough quarters to call Elio. I dialed his phone number and waited for his phone to connect. He answered on the first ring, and I paused as I heard the familiar softness of his voice, "Hello." I stood in silence and his voice repeated, "Hello?"

I waited with an endless hope that somehow, he would save me from my life. I wanted him to want me. I longed for him to make everything better, to take me in, and love me forever. I waited for happily ever after. I wanted him to say the words.

I recalled jogging down the sandy path to the San Francisco Bay. I observed the seagulls spiraling down and swirling above. I interjected the jet airliners landing at Oakland airport, and I beheld Elio's eyes looking down at me. Andy Warhol and his soup cans lingered, while R2-D2 spun in confusion. I hungered for him, and I heard Elio hang up the receiver. I listened to the faint sound of vehicles passing by on the highway.

My logic reminded me; I was still a married woman, and I had a long runway ahead of me. "I will need time alone. I need to figure out what I will do, and where I will go," I told myself. I pounded my head against the phone booth door. "What am I thinking?" I asked myself. *Why can I not tell him my true feelings?*

I hung up the receiver and returned to the small space in my car. It dawned on me that I was starting over again, except this time, my vehicle was packed with more than two suitcases.

My thoughts raced in and out. *"I love him,"* I told myself, "But I am married to Arthur." I twisted around highway corners, while skiers zipped by me on straight stretches. I noticed small specks of snow fell, landing on my windshield. The ground beneath caught the light dusting of white. My Volkswagen maneuvered with ease through the conditions, as I continued my journey higher up the mountain, and into snow country.

THE PALMS OF MY HANDS WERE SWEATY, AND MY HEART POUNDED. I slowly entered my duplex and picked up the last item to carry out to my car. Arthur was sitting on the couch and refused to speak to me. I looked at him for the last time. My heart ached, and I couldn't help feeling guilty for leaving. "It's time for me to go, I have a very long drive ahead of me, and I must move on." Arthur sat in silence as I walked over and extended a hand. Instead, he rose and held me tightly.

I was frigid, my arms remained by my side. He finally released me, and I briskly walked away. "Drive safe Tess, I love you," Arthur's words faded, along with the distant memory of my childhood home.

I backed out the driveway and shifted into first gear. I pressed the gas pedal and shifted into second, and then third. I entered the main boulevard and shifted into fourth gear. I started smiling, my knees shook, and my smile grew bigger and bigger. I felt free. I felt like I could fly.

SNOWFLAKES TURNED INTO SNOW, LOTS OF SNOW. MY WINDSHIELD wipers continued to move slowly back and forth across my windshield. The pine tree branches were heavier, and as I looked in my rear-view mirror, I saw only my single trail of tire tracks behind me. "I am close," I told myself. I turned off Highway 88 and drove down the majestic road leading to my parent's home. As their cabin came into view, I shifted down in gear, and slowed to a stop.

My radio crackled and picked up a distant radio reception. I heard the faded voice of Joni Mitchell. I turned up the volume, soaking up her falsetto voice, and lit myself a cigarette. I watched as the flame of the match seemed to explode on the first strike, and as I inhaled, her words flowed, and my eyes watered. The song "Both Sides Now" had new meaning, and I felt as though she was singing my life; reminding me of Bogota and the small transistor radio. I paid close attention to her words.

I stared at my parent's home in the mountains, and I remembered the good times we spent in our family cabin. I thought of Arthur, and our countless weekends here. Arthur and I would ski on every run at nearby Kirkwood Ski Resort. We were competitive skiers, and I had mastered the art quite well.

This music caused memories to rush in. I heard the tempo of the music, and I saw a metronome swing back and forth. My dance instructor repeated, one, two, three, one, two, three. My uncle's wooden bird swung up and down into the glass of water, while their other bird rested upon my finger.

I saw myself dancing at the boys' club, the grammar school dances, and admiring the Battle of the Bands. My mind captured Andre and I at his prom, as he took my hand and held me close. There was the dance with Luis, on the beach in Brazil, his green eyes, and his whisper. Then, my dance with Arthur on our wedding day, and my hopes for our future. And finally, my last dance with Elio. The connection, the electricity that flowed through my finger-tips, his touch and kisses.

I watched as the smoke rose from the chimney, circling up and into the sky. I rolled down my window and smelled the burning of dry pine wood. Father always preferred to burn pine. It burns hot and fast. I continued smoking my cigarette, and listened while my eyes scanned the outline of the roof, and the tops of the trees. The clouds lingered as the sunlight streamed down between each stratus layer.

I opened my car door, and stepped outside into ankle deep snow. The sound of my shoes against its crust crunched with each step. I exhaled, and a fine mist flowed from my mouth, dissipating before my eyes. I grabbed my purse and jacket and looked up one last time, into the afternoon sky. It was a crisp day, cold, and it had just the right amount of energy. Heavy snow had turned into feather light wisps, dancing back and forth.

I closed my door and slowly descended the countless steps leading to my parent's front porch. I counted each one. I noticed the water wheel, with a frozen pond beneath it. I heard and smelled the air as it passed my face, and beyond into eternity. It whispered to me, "Fly, Tess, fly."

I hesitated as I stood in front of the entry door. I gently tapped on the window. From inside the house, I heard my Mother holler: "Tess is here, Tess is home."

ACKNOWLEDGMENTS

I would like to thank the following persons for their tremendous support, hours of conversations, and much needed help while making this book happen:

The Class of 74 girlfriends; you know who you are! We continue to get together and solve the world's problems!

Thank you Dave & Dori, Joe & Debbie, along with my Napa Valley community friends.

Thanks to Linda, Jill & Lorrie, whom I worked countless hours beside and who continue to support my writing,

My brother Albert and my sister Jessica, who listened to my every concern, thank you so much.

And, to Stacey my editor. She held me up during numerous shadows of doubt, and who guided me through my deepest of waters.

Thank you

ABOUT THE AUTHOR

Tess Hamilton's desire to write began as a child. Her father would share his exceptional imagination and his love and encouragement for Tess to pursue her dreams, however distant they may seem. While he pounded away on his manual typewriter, striking each key with intense enthusiasm along with a particular gleam in his eyes, he entranced Tess. His image is firmly embedded in her memory forever.

After navigating across numerous thresholds, Tess finally devoted countless hours into writing her own journey. Surrounded in solitude, sharing that gleam in her own eyes, and striking her keyboard with her own intense enthusiasm, Tess's efforts blossomed into her first novel, *Thoughts of Leaving*.

Tess currently resides in Wyoming and is writing her second book, a sequel entitled *Thoughts of Leaving Reappear*.

f facebook.com/Thoughtsofleaving

Made in the USA
Las Vegas, NV
09 August 2021